This compilation of Steve Gerkin's evocative stories is some of the best writing I have read in a very long time. Each one is a gem and when strung together the reader will find an exquisite literary necklace.
—*Michael Wallis*
author, historian, human geographer

In Hidden History of Tulsa, Steve Gerkin does a masterful job of reclaiming some of the city's most remarkable stories and preserving them for a new generation of Oklahomans. Together, these tales of injustice and triumph, opportunism and creativity, give us a broader, deeper understanding of who we are, not just as a community but also as citizens of a complex yet wondrous world.
—*Teresa Miller, executive director*
Oklahoma Center for Poets and Writers
Oklahoma State University–Tulsa

History presents a correlation between our lives today and those who have gone before us. Gerkin's stories prompt us to explore some of Tulsa's tales of tragedy and triumph as well as calamity and recovery. We must ask ourselves the following: How did this happen? Could it happen again? How far have we come?
—*S. Michelle Place, executive director*
Tulsa Historical Society

Tulsa has a rich history—some great and some not so great—but there is much that can be gleaned from stories that may not make the history books. Dr. Gerkin has created a very readable work that brings to life, through stories most people never knew, that part of our history, which might otherwise be lost.
—*Howard G. Barnett, Jr., president*
Oklahoma State University–Tulsa

This well-written and informative book about Tulsa's "hidden" history reveals the not-so-well-known people, places and events that shaped the history of this great community. In this entertaining tome, you will discover many interesting and some heartbreaking stories about Tulsa.
—*Beth Freeman, director*
Oklahoma State University–Tulsa Library and Archives

HIDDEN
HISTORY
of
TULSA

Steve Gerkin

THE
History
PRESS

Published by The History Press
Charleston, SC 29403
www.historypress.net

First published 2014

ISBN 978.1.5402.1070.8

Library of Congress Cataloging-in-Publication Data

Gerkin, Steve.
Hidden history of Tulsa / Steve Gerkin.
pages cm.
Includes bibliographical references.
ISBN 978-1-62619-579-0
1. Tulsa (Okla.)--History. 2. Tulsa (Okla.)--Biography. I. Title.
F704.T92G47 2014
976.6'86--dc23
2014017144

This first book is dedicated to my wife, Sue—my true love, a lady who loves me back.

CONTENTS

CONTENTS

PROLOGUE

Built along the Arkansas River, the late-1800s cow town of Tulsa became the world's biggest oil slick. Rowdies, roughnecks and renegades descended on the overnight oil industry. For decades, Tulsa was touted as the "Oil Capital of the World." These and other known historical events about "Tulsey Town" have been above ground for years. Yet there are also hidden, historical nuggets right below the surface.

Colorful personalities, racial chaos and criminals, both white collar and blue, dotted the developing landscape. Shrouded by the glitter and wealth generated from the oil industry and the coming of Oral Roberts to south Tulsa, the forgotten history of Tulsa went underground.

Tragedies and triumphs colorize the fabric of any community. Tulsa has had an abundance of fascinating folk who provided a human infrastructure of intrigue, glory and mayhem.

The Ku Klux Klan dominated the political and legal venues in the 1910s and '20s. It influenced elections, verdicts and racial tensions. Blacks migrating from southern slavery states and black freedmen from Oklahoma tribes organized a highly developed black community on the north side of the downtown tracks. Named Greenwood, this settlement earned the title of Black Wall Street. The race riot of 1921 is no secret—at least, not any more. Exposed on these pages are the hidden truths and the horrors of several of the massacre's victims.

Outrageous professional wrestlers took center stage at the downtown entertainment emporium known as the Avey Coliseum. Clowns and

Hollywood entertainers graced the stage along Sixth Street, a street also known as Cedar Street, Tulsa's proudest thoroughfare for decades that is born again in today's Pearl District.

Trolleys transported Tulsans to the Coliseum, fairgrounds and the Cains Ballroom to hear the likes of western swing rivals Bob Wills and the murderous maestro Spade Cooley, whose oversized pictures look down on the ballroom floor.

The exposure of the veiled episodes of Tulsa, set free from seclusion, provides an evocative and enjoyable voyage through its hidden history.

ACKNOWLEDGEMENTS

The journey to write historical pieces about the Tulsa area became an eye-opening adventure. Many people deserve hearty thanks.

With one exception, the essays in this book appeared in *This Land* magazine, found at thislandpress.com. *This Land* offered a cub reporter a chance to be published. As a contributing editor for *This Land*, I am especially grateful for the editorial marshaling of *This Land* founder and editor Michael Mason and Mark Brown, as well as, Vince Lovoi, publisher.

Literary inspiration lies with my good friend, author and human geographer Michael Wallis, who encourages me to search for tantalizing tales and spin songdog stories.

Exhaustive research is key to historical writing. Without the talented Sheri Perkins of the Tulsa Public Library, many of these stories would be lacking.

Images on these pages are, generally, from olden times and require a team of photo gurus like Marc Carlson of the Tulsa University's Special Collections and University Archives, Ian Swart of the Tulsa Historical Society and Kathryn Red Corn of the Osage Tribal Museum.

Debbie Neece, Lynn Watts, Beth Freeman and Carol Fillmore were instrumental in providing and improving critical images, as were the Rudisill Regional Library and the Booker T. Washington High School Library. Jim and Chad Rodgers opened the doors of Tulsa's Cains Ballroom so that I could capture Spade Cooley on film.

Most of my articles are about people long gone. Yet a few are still vertical and were real champions to tolerate my questions and taunts.

Acknowledgements

Major thanks go to the precious Perlie Moreland, the inimitable J.J. Conley, the resilient K. Rahall, hay artisan Kelly Cox and bad boy turned preacher Johnny Lee Clary.

Thanks, too, for the gracious comments of Michael Wallis, Teresa Miller, Howard Barnett, Beth Freeman and Michelle Place.

Lastly, I salute the Iowa Public School System for giving me a good grammar background.

Part I

EARLY RACIAL TENSIONS:
TULSA RACE RIOT OF 1921 AND THE PRESENCE OF WHITE SUPREMACISTS

Chapter 1

BENO HALL

Tulsa's Den of Terror

T he monstrous, three-story, steel-reinforced stucco building towered along the western edge of Greenwood. It dominated the landscape at the foot of Standpipe Hill, sporting a bright whitewash, the favorite color of its primary residents. Inside, its members vowed to protect their notion of "100% Americanism." To become a guardian of liberty, they reasoned, you had to swear to secrecy and seclusion. And you had to embrace intimidation and violence as a way to assert your values.

In January 1922, the Tulsa Benevolent Association of Tulsa, Oklahoma, was officially formed as a holding company for the Knights of the Ku Klux Klan, Incorporated. Among its founding members was Washington E. Hudson, the attorney for Dick Rowland, the young black who was a scapegoat for the 1921 Tulsa race riot. They provided the financing and leadership to begin building their Klan temple, or Klavern, known as Beno Hall. Locals jokingly called it "Be No Hall" as in "Be No Nigger, Be No Jew, Be No Catholic, Be No Immigrant."

Six months after its inception and bolstered by a raffle of thirteen Ford automobiles netting nearly half of the $60,000 purchase price of the building, the Benevolent Association bought the Centenary Methodist Church, at 501 North Main Street—at North Main and Easton Streets. The organization quickly outgrew this facility, and the church was razed, making way for the future monument of white supremacy. Beno Hall was built for $200,000 ($1.5 million in today's currency). Financing of the construction was kept quiet, but entrepreneur, politician and early booster of Tulsa Tate Brady and his wife, Rachel Brady, who received a large parcel as a Cherokee allotment in 1910, owned the land. When Beno Hall was completed, it was one of the largest auditoriums in the Southwest, holding three thousand people. Its size alone provided Tulsa with a visual reminder of the Invisible Empire's power, passion and presence.

Abundant evidence points the finger at the Klan for fanning the sociological tinderbox that was 1920s Tulsa. Yearning for a spark—even an invented one—a fired-up mob of whites took the bait and burned Greenwood to the ground in the Memorial Day 1921 race riot. Two months later, a national Klan official, Caleb Ridley, who was also a Baptist minister, lectured at the Tulsa Convention Hall on the principles of the Klan, calling the riot a complete success, adding that it "was the best thing to ever happen to Tulsa and that judging from the way strange Negroes were coming to Tulsa we might have to do it all over again."

Under the watchful eye of its Tulsa leader, the Exalted Cyclops William Shelley Rogers, membership grew to include all civic and social levels, from law enforcement to welders, bankers, dry cleaners, judges, commissioners and oil field workers. All partook in the Beno Hall sessions that focused on increasing membership and efforts to keep Tulsa free from moral corruption and centered on family values.

A fiery induction of Ku Klux Klan members. *Oklahoma State University, Tulsa Campus Library, Ruth Sigler Avery Tulsa Race Riot Archives.*

Barely three months after the riot, some 300 Tulsans, supported by a throng of 1,500 onlookers, were initiated as the first class of the Tulsa Klan No. 2. A year later, in a field north of Owasso, a nighttime "naturalization" ceremony initiated 1,020 Tulsa Klavern members before a fiery, seventy-by-twenty-foot cross.

Recruiters known as Kleagles "capitalized upon the emotions in the wake of the race riot to propagandize the white community of Tulsa," writes Carter Blue Clark in his 1976 dissertation, *A History of the Ku Klux Klan in Oklahoma.* While the Oklahoma Klan boasted over 150,000 hooded devotees in the early 1920s, the Tulsa Klavern—a reference to the smallest local unit of the organizational structure, wherein ritual ceremonies and Klan Khoral Klub rehearsals were held—swelled to 3,000 members. Hence, the group needed a permanent structure—a very large, secure structure.

Nestled near the one-year-old ashes of upper-class black homes that once sprawled up the slopes of Sunset and Standpipe Hills, overlooking the industry that was Greenwood, Beno Hall towered over nearly two thousand black Tulsans as they huddled in makeshift tents. They lived within earshot of the member revelry. From the halls of Beno sprung midnight parades; cross burnings along the boundaries of Greenwood; night-riding terrors; meetings determining political candidates' success or failure; and plans to squash the proliferation of filthy people with filthy morals who bootlegged, gambled, consorted with whores or were unfaithful husbands—all of which conflicted with the Klan's version of white, Protestant ideology.

The Klan loved parades. The most spectacular occurred in August 1922, while the wounds of the 1921 riot were still fresh. The parade featured 1,741 white-robed members marching silently through downtown Tulsa before an estimated crowd of fifteen thousand. The women's auxiliary of the Klan provided extra pizzazz, carrying signs with various slogans such as "Kiss the flag or cross the pond," a reminder that immigrants were not Americans and therefore there should "be no(ne)" on American soil, certainly not in Oklahoma.

The Knights had nothing against what they deemed "good niggers." They were morally incensed by the behavior of some white men—especially the oil field workers who used the trolley system to come to downtown Tulsa, where they spent their cash on booze, dames and pounds of cocaine, morphine and heroin. In *Tulsa: Biography of the American City,* Danney Goble wrote, "Kluxers meted out rough justice to those that lived beyond the law's bounds"—justice that predominantly involved acts against white Protestants.

The Klan wasn't just for older white men, either. The Tulsa Klavern vigorously promoted women's participation within the Klan society and an

The Tulsa Klan paraded from Beno Hall through the former riot section of town. *Beryl Ford Collection/Rotary Club and Tulsa Historical Society.*

adolescent male branch called the Junior Ku Klux Klan, which recruited boys aged twelve to eighteen.

According to an invitation on Junior Ku Klux Klan stationery from the Tulsa Benevolent Association, a Junior KKK "Open Air Initiation" at the Lynch Farm north of Rose Hill Cemetery began at 7:30 p.m. on Friday, September 18, 1924. It promised a ride to the event, if needed, and "lots of fireworks."

When the seasons turned chilly, Beno Hall became the Junior Klan's initiation site. On January 22, 1925, "all members were expected to be there, members received $.50 for each candidate they bring and new initiates must pay at least $2 on his initiation." The same invitation announced a party sponsored by the men's branch of the Klan, stating the "Final Plans for the Big Weiner and Marshmallow Roast on Thursday night, January 29, when you can bring your girl." The attraction of the evening proved to be a talk by the assistant to the Exalted Cyclops and "ice cream sandwiches—O Boy!"

Beno Hall supplied new recruits with official Klan gear. For a premium price, reportedly pocketed by national officials, the home office in Atlanta regularly shipped cheap, white sheets and pointed hats, all with the tightly sewn-on patch of the organization. Yet a Tulsa Knight's trappings were incomplete without the Klan weapon of choice, the official KKK whipping strap.

The strap was a piece of top-grain leather four inches wide and three feet long, with the handle wrapped in industrial tape and its last six inches cut into ten slits, effective for slicing through skin. Hundreds of these prized weapons arrived in Tulsa.

During the Oklahoma Klan heyday years between 1921 and 1924, officials knew of 102 Klan floggings, three killings, three mutilations (including castrations) and numerous instances of people being tarred and feathered, which, as a rule, followed whippings of the victims' backs. Official but incomplete tallies showed that Tulsa County provided the most violations with 74, and Okmulgee County chalked up 20, while the rest of the state totaled 37.

At the time, lawlessness prevailed in Tulsa. A local reporter witnessed the flogging of J.E. Fletcher, an alleged car thief and bootlegger, on a remote Sand Springs road in September 1921. County Attorney John Seaver said no inquiry would be made, that Fletcher had gotten what he deserved and an investigation would just lead to criticism of the investigators. This gave carte blanche to extralegal marauding.

During that same month, a statement by H.O. McClure, president of the Tulsa Chamber of Commerce, put the writing on the wall in a *Tulsa World* article: "In Tulsa our courthouse and city hall are practically filled with Klan members, elected to office with Klan support." It wouldn't be long before an Oklahoma governor would step in to throttle the free hand of Tulsa's hooded fraternity.

After local Klansmen used their whipping straps to mutilate the genitalia of accused drug peddler Nathan Hantaman, the already unpopular governor Jack Walton on August 14, 1923, declared martial law in the city and county of Tulsa. The results of the military court investigation drew statewide attention to the horror of the Oklahoma extremists as twelve locals were hauled away. The Oklahoma legislature passed an anti-mask bill hoping to stem vigilante violence.

The flamboyant Walton, aiming squarely at the Tulsa Klavern, even calling it by name, went on the attack, saying, "I don't care if you burst right into them with a double-barreled shot gun. I'll promise you a pardon in advance." Additional irresponsible statements, the suspension of the writ of habeas corpus, censorship of the press, an effective Klan defense and counterattack and the extension of military rule to include the entire state further weakened public sentiment toward the state's leader.

Governor Walton's declaration of war on the Order exposed its reign of terror, but the Klan would get the last laugh. The supremacists influenced the impeachment of "Jazz Band Jack" Walton, who served but ten months as governor. The boys in white cheered the demise of their nemesis in their newly dedicated Beno Hall that had earlier been the site of a Tri-State Klan convention.

The next few years saw a healthy Klavern using its North Tulsa facility for holiday dances, ice cream socials and political plotting. The outer foliage appeared robust, but inside, the society was withering from internal disagreements, greed and graft. By 1928, the Oklahoma Klan had negligible power.

The Tulsa Benevolent Association sold the storied building to the Temple Baptist Church in 1930. During the Depression, the building housed a speakeasy, then a skating rink, then a lumberyard and finally a dance hall before radio evangelist Steve Pringle turned it into the Evangelistic Temple of the First Pentecostal Church. In his first revival meeting, Pringle

The Evangelistic Church was the last occupant of Beno Hall, the former KKK clubhouse. *Ruth Sigler Avery, OSU–Tulsa Special Collections and Archives.*

introduced a little-known Enid preacher by the name of Oral Roberts, who worked his animated, faith-healing magic on the bare lot next door. Roberts impressed in the tent atmosphere and preached with his cohort inside the vast auditorium once known as Beno Hall. His fire and brimstone was a fitting bookend to the fiery crusades of the Klan.

Throughout the seventies, Beno Hall became a Main Street blight where vagrants gambled, drug transactions took place and sex was exchanged for money. It was destroyed in 1976, and the empty lot now belongs to the Oklahoma Department of Highways.

Chapter 2

THE WHITE KNIGHT VIGILANTES

Exposing the Founders of Tulsa's Ku Klux Klan Clubhouse

The attorney smelled good. Damie Roland remembered certain things about her son's court-appointed attorney, Washington Elias Hudson, known around town simply as "Wash." The squeaky-voiced, bowtie-wearing Hudson sported prominent ears and a neatly trimmed moustache, providing fodder for numerous cartoon caricatures. He had an intense look, one that the Rolands might have found reassuring.

Dick Roland was a young black man who was questionably accused of assault with intent to rape a white seventeen-year-old named Sarah Page. Yellow newspapermen used Roland's arrest in their reporting, which many argued helped provoke the deadly Tulsa race riot of 1921. Much of Tulsa seemed anxious to get ahold of Roland. A prominent Vanderbilt-trained attorney and a successful state politician, Hudson was in many respects the ideal lawyer for Roland—with one glaring exception.

Wash Hudson was the leader of Oklahoma's Ku Klux Klan.

Hudson's father served as a Cyclops in the Tennessee Klan following the Civil War. Wash saw Tulsa as a lawless city and relished the chance to lead the Klan as an opportunity to fight crime. "The law had broken down completely," Hudson recalled in a 1960 *Tulsa Tribune* article. "Women were raped on the streets. Men were robbed." He continued, "We cleaned things up."

Dick Roland disappeared. Damie, Dick's adoptive mother, claims Sheriff McCollough told her that officers took him to friends of Sarah Page's in Kansas City—to keep him safe from a lynch mob. But there are few traces of his existence afterwards. With some blacks infuriated with him, Dick's time in

Tulsa was over while the Klan gained momentum.

Wash Hudson decided to do the unthinkable, despite the racial tension. Instead of backing away from the Klan, he, along with several important Tulsans, decided to make it official.

All five of the white trustees of the Tulsa Benevolent Association (TBA) were pillars of the city: Wash E. Hudson (chairman), John Rogers (secretary), C.W. Benedict, William "Shelley" Rogers and Alf G. Heggem (the latter three as trustees). On January 5, 1922, they signed the articles of incorporation for the Tulsa Benevolent Association, which officially established the Ku Klux Klan as a legal organization in the state of Oklahoma. The Tulsa KKK was born a mere six months after the Tulsa race riot.

Washington Hudson was a former head of the Oklahoma KKK, president of the Tulsa Benevolent Association and founder of the Tulsa Law School. *From* History of Oklahoma, *vol. 3.*

But who, precisely, were the fathers of Tulsa's Klan? Wash Hudson, Roland's attorney, served as a state legislator and founder of the Tulsa Law School, while John Rogers, a future dean of the University of Tulsa College of Law, served as general counsel for McMan Oil company. Heggem was a well-respected mechanical engineer, Benedict was a banker and Shelley Rogers was a private attorney. Three of the men worked in the First National Bank building in Downtown Tulsa.

The first office of the Tulsa Benevolent Association was listed as the second floor of the Mayo Building at 420 South Main. Yet, the confined nature of the location would not suffice for such a popular organization. Overwhelmed with a tsunami of new initiates following the riot, the Klan founders moved to secure a Klan Klubhouse. They bought Centenary Methodist-Episcopal Church, located on the edge of the riot scene, but even the new accommodations could not contain the rapidly growing membership. In 1923, they erected a three-thousand-seat, white plaster behemoth for meetings. Locals called it "Be-No Hall," as in "Be No Niggers, Be No Jews, Be No Catholics, Be No Immigrants." The monolith of menace at 501 North Main stood above the ashes of the former dwellings of race riot survivors and overlooked the tents that had replaced their homes.

The Tulsa Benevolent Association wasn't the only extremist group in town; vigilante squads became authorized law enforcement. Organized under the supervision of Tulsa County sheriff and Klan member W.M. McCollough, the Tulsa Law Enforcement Club was established on a cold December 1921 night during a citizen's mass meeting at the First Baptist Church. The club selected five men, including TBA officials John Rogers and Alf Heggem, to wage war with the criminal community and eradicate the bordellos, "Choc" beer joints and dope dens of Tulsa County. This commission and its representatives, along with County Attorney William Seaver and several justices, crafted guidelines that produced a cleanup squad of nightriders, whose responsibility was to systematically purge the immoral element of Tulsa—much of which they believed was located in Greenwood.

Beno Hall, according to Tulsa historian David Breed, "was the launching point of midnight parades, and they would bring crosses and burn them along the boundaries of the Greenwood district." Twenty-three Tulsa KKK Knights were charged with civic rioting and assaults as nightriders with their own brand of moral cleansing. Downtown Tulsa parades of sign-toting Klansmen, Klanswomen and Klan Juniors marched in their regalia. According to a Tulsa police history, 1,741 Klan members in full regalia marched through downtown on April 1, 1922. The empire's presence in state and local politics was undeniable.

Three of five Tulsa County state representatives in 1923 were admitted Klansmen. Political meetings at Beno yielded a slate of candidates that won the local municipal elections in 1924. Several association founders were instrumental in the legal community.

In addition to founding a civic club for white Knights, Wash Hudson yearned for a law school in Tulsa. Together with four other attorneys that included his son, Hudson was granted a state charter in 1923 to open the Tulsa Law School, a freestanding school with no educational institution affiliation. Hudson became the first dean and taught those first years in the basement of Central High School. For twenty years, Wash loaned his name to the school, but he sought a collegiate relationship for the law school. John Rogers and Hudson found another common, civic bond.

While serving on the University of Tulsa (TU) Board of Trustees and as chair of its Committee on Faculty and Curriculum, Rogers squired the acquisition of Hudson's law school into the university family, creating the University of Tulsa College of Law in 1943. E.E. Hanson ran the school from his Mayo Building office, while Rogers served as a strong-handed overseer. Bruce Peterson, once a professor and dean of the law school, maintained, "You did not sneeze without Mr. Roger's permission."

John Rogers became the official dean of the TU law school in 1949. Several years later, a racial episode surfaced when Kenneth Dones, an African American and the son-in-law of Edwin Goodwin, publisher of the Tulsa black-owned newspaper *Oklahoma Eagle*, applied for admission. Some say Kenneth's application was slightly late, so Rogers did not admit him but rather allowed him to audit the first year if he promised to transfer to another law school the next

John Rogers was a prominent Tulsa attorney whose brief membership in the Klan included a position on the Tulsa Benevolent Association. *From* History of Oklahoma at the Golden Anniversary of Statehood, *37.*

year. Dones completed his law degree at Washburn University. *Oklahoma Eagle* publisher Goodwin applied successfully in 1958 to the TU College of Law, gaining admittance without a hint of discrimination. The Klan, by then, had lost its clout.

What would drive a man like Rogers to help establish the Tulsa Benevolent Association? He was clearly a joiner. Rogers was instrumental in the formation of the Oklahoma American Legion and the Tulsa YMCA, served as chamber of commerce president in 1936, was a University of Oklahoma regent and held multiple University of Tulsa positions while creating the Tulsa Council of Churches. Outside of his wife and son, the First Christian Church in Tulsa and its national organization were the focal points of his life. Along with other TBA trustees, his positive contributions to the Tulsa community are unquestioned and significant.

While Rogers's membership in the Klan was ill chosen and short-lived, Wash Hudson's involvement was more complicated. Throughout his tenure as a

Democrat in the Oklahoma State House of Representatives (1915–17) and Senate (1923–27), Hudson was open regarding his Klan affiliation. During his first year as a senator, Hudson became the majority (Democratic) floor leader who prepared and presented a successful impeachment charge against Governor Jack Walton, a known opponent of the Invisible Empire, who referred to the Klan as "that whipping crowd," while offering "a pardon in advance if you burst right into them with a double-barreled shot gun." The November 1923 regular meeting at the recently dedicated Beno Hall celebrated the ouster of "Jazz Band Jack" Walton.

In 1924, a Klansman from the east speaking at Beno Hall promoted a stand against Catholics, Jews and Negroes. This rhetoric sharply contrasted with the assurance given by a national Klansman, who recruited Hudson several years earlier, that the Klan oath had nothing religious about it. Hudson retorted with his own fiery speech and quit the organization, nearly causing uproar. He claimed the entire Klan organization was under the direction of the national Republican committee. Subsequently, the Grand Dragon of the Oklahoma Klan, N.C. Jewett, banished Hudson. After a change in the leadership of the Oklahoma Realm, Wash, along with his son Robert D. Hudson, rejoined the Tulsa Klavern, although the organization was in a gradual decline and his friend John Rogers was no longer on the rolls. The diminutive Hudson continued marching to the Klan klubhouse until the bitter end.

And what became of the other three founders of the Tulsa Benevolent Association? Klan member and mechanical engineer Alf G. Heggem was one of the original directors of the International Petroleum Exposition that brought thousands of oil-related professionals to Tulsa. The Tulsa Chamber of Commerce magazine, *Tulsa Spirit*, described Alf as an "apostle with keen business sense." Heggem supported the Trinity Episcopal Church, served as the chamber's president in 1927 and belonged to the Rotary Club and assorted Masonic rites. The Norwegian descendant was issued numerous patents for his gas preservation inventions and made a fortune, primarily from the Cushing oil field bonanza rather than lawyering, like the other TBA founders.

With offices in the First National Bank Building, attorney William Shelley Rogers led the Tulsa Klavern as the Exalted Cyclops at the time of the Benevolent Association's creation, succeeding Wash as the corporation's chairman. Living on Fifteenth Street just shy of Utica, across from the current location of Panera Bread, Shelley orchestrated the activities of the Junior KKK for teenage boys, the Khoral Klub and the Klan's women's auxiliary. He also organized dances and ice cream socials held in Beno Hall.

Serving years as a vice-president of the First National Bank in Tulsa, Klansman Channing W. Benedict and his wife headed south by 1940, when he

Channing Benedict, Tulsa Benevolent Association board member, retired to Houston as the owner of the Chief Motel. *Author collection from cardcow.com.*

became the manager of a camp in Harris, Texas, and the last manager of the Chief Motel in Houston. While Benedict was content simply to practice law in Tulsa, Wash Hudson and John Rogers shared much larger aspirations.

They ran against each other for the Oklahoma State Senate in 1922. With the strong, Democratic, political clout of the Klan behind Hudson, the Republican Rogers was soundly defeated, later joking that he had the Klan to thank for keeping him out of politics.

By 1925, the Tulsa Benevolent Association ceased to exist. The departure of Wash and other prominent Knights who objected to the Klan pressuring members to change their party affiliation to Republican deflated the empire's stature. Internal politics became a death knell for the Tulsa Klan.

With a withering membership and decline in political panache, Beno Hall became insolvent by 1929, becoming property of the sheriff of Tulsa County. The Evangelistic Temple of the First Pentecostal (Baptist) Church of evangelist and old-time-religion radio personality Steve Pringle bought the Sheriff Deed to the infamous Beno Hall property, where a spirited, young preacher from Enid, Oral Roberts, joined the ministry, preaching his first tent revival alongside the Temple at the base of Standpipe Hill.

The former Tulsa Benevolent Association building became a social blight in the early 1970s, providing space for entrepreneurs of the flesh and drug trade. Purchased by the Oklahoma Highway Department for freeway right of way, the building was demolished, leaving a vacant lot today where the former Klan and its leaders once terrorized the city.

Chapter 3

WATTS AND CLARY

The Odd Couple of Civil Rights Reconciliation

Dressed only in his boxers, Wade Watts, a black civil rights activist reclined on the sofa. He read the morning paper while bacon, eggs and pork sausage sizzled in the kitchen. The cook leaned into the living room doorway.

"Do you think your friend Martin Luther King, who dreamt that one day, blacks and whites could come together, ever imagined it might include us?"

Johnny Lee Clary, the former Imperial Wizard of the White Knights of the Ku Klux Klan, returned to the stove.

From the other room, Watts, an evangelist and long-time leader of the NAACP, shouted his answer.

"No," he said, "I don't believe the dream would have gone that far. But don't burn this couch after I leave, honky."

A few years earlier, that may have been a possibility. While Johnny Lee was the Grand Dragon of the Oklahoma Klan, the Klan set fire to Watts's church, nearly burning it to the ground.

As the Grand Dragon of Oklahoma, Clary launched an all-out campaign of retribution against the disciple of love, the Reverend Watts. During a late 1970s radio debate in Oklahoma City, Watts tormented Clary, citing scripture and sprinkling his rebuttals with "Jesus loves you." Embarrassed Klan protégées listened to the destruction of Johnny Lee.

Wade Watts was born in the hills of Kiamichi, in southeast Oklahoma, in 1919. Indoctrinated into the teachings of the Baptist church at a young age, he committed his life to Christian ideals. At seventeen, Watts joined the NAACP.

The organization elected him the state president in 1968, a position he held for sixteen years. His respect within the civil rights community escalated as he fought for desegregation of public facilities and institutions during the 1940s and 1950s, including his work with Justice Thurgood Marshall, which paved the way for a Supreme Court decision to allow admittance of a black woman, Ada Lois Sipuel, to the University of Oklahoma law school in 1949, where she was required to sit alone in class behind a sign that said "colored." She ate in a section of the cafeteria cordoned by a chain so she could not mix with white students.

Watts fought hard within Oklahoma to ensure that blacks were given equal educational opportunities through segregation in the public school system. His efforts benefited his nephew Julius Caesar Watts, who was educated in the newly integrated schools in Eufaula. J.C., as he was known, became a national-class quarterback for the University of Oklahoma, and he was free to saunter the campus unencumbered by racial boundaries.

In 1965, Wade Watts marched with his good friend Martin Luther King in the Selma, Alabama demonstration for racial freedom, justice and equality. President Lyndon Johnson appointed Watts to the Civil Rights Commission. Within his home state, he served on the Human Rights Commission while maintaining his day job as labor inspector for the Oklahoma State Labor Commission. His passion for racial acceptance started at an early age—after his first exposure to hate.

As a young boy, Wade played with a white companion who invited him home for lunch. He was not allowed to sit at the table; instead, he was led to the back porch where the mother handed him a bowl of food. The family dog became incensed with Watts, barking and trying to bite him. His friend explained the dog was

Wade Watts, the former head of the Oklahoma NAACP and a McAlester, Oklahoma preacher, converted Klan Wizard Johnny Lee Clary, and the two teamed up for a lifelong friendship. *Lynn Watts photo.*

mad that Watts was eating out of his dish. This would not be the last time a plate of food reminded him of racial discrimination.

In the late 1950s, Watts and his good friend, the powerful Oklahoma state senator Gene Stipe, entered an Ada cafe for lunch. The waitress stopped them, saying, "We don't serve Negroes." Wade responded, "I don't eat Negroes. I just came to get some ham and eggs." Leaving the establishment, Stipes asked Watts if God would grant him one wish, what would it be. The senator anticipated that his companion might wish for no more hate in the world. Without hesitation, Watts said he wanted to meet the leader of the Ku Klux Klan.

In a small San Francisco suburb, during this time period, Johnny Lee Clary was born into a hate-mongering environment. Soon after his birth, the Clary family returned to their small, central Oklahoma hometown of Del City, a predominantly all-white city. His bigoted daddy continued his hardworking ways, while his alcoholic mother strayed with multiple lovers. Johnny Lee's dad taught him that those were not "chocolate-covered" men but "niggers." Clary's Uncle Harold bragged that he shot a black man for crossing his yard and only got fined for firing a gun within the city limits.

At age eleven, Clary walked into the house and witnessed his father's suicide. Just as Clary screamed, "Don't do it," his dad put a forty-five-caliber slug into his head. Mom moved in with her boyfriend, who beat the traumatized youngster, prompting Clary to complain to the police. After law enforcement threatened the couple with jail, the boyfriend delivered the ultimatum of either Clary or him staying. His mother kicked Johnny out of the house. The tough kid ended up with an older sister in gang-laden Los Angeles, where the beatings continued at the hand of her lover. A despondent Clary desperately wanted a family that wanted him.

Watching TV one afternoon, Clary found it. The interviewer was questioning David Duke, the Imperial Wizard of the Ku Klux Klan. Recalling Uncle Harold's story, Clary contacted the Klan. An emissary of Duke knocked on his door several weeks later.

The KKK recruiter told him the Klan was a family with a spiritual basis and took him to weekly meetings where people who wanted to hear what he had to say surrounded the teenager. He diligently studied the Klan. He trembled with excitement on the day he was officially inducted. Clary was fourteen. With his new support system's guidance, he had learned how to hate. Clary ascended the Klan ranks quickly.

His brute physicality made him a natural as David Duke's bodyguard. His charismatic persona led to a position as an overly ambitious Kleagle or Klan membership recruiter in Del City. At the not-so-tender age of twenty-one,

Johnny Lee was the leader of the Oklahoma Klan as the Grand Dragon, Clary was on the career path he desired—Imperial Wizard of the KKK.

In 1979, an Oklahoma City radio host invited Clary to participate in an on-air debate with a black man. Licking his chops at "a chance to put a black man in his place," Grand Dragon Clary jumped at the chance to spread the gospel of hate. Clary told all his buddies to tune in. His debate opponent was the Reverend Wade Watts, veteran pastor of the Jerusalem Baptist Church in McAlester, Oklahoma.

As the two approached each other for the 1979 broadcast, Clary was shocked. "He caught me off guard," Clary told an Australian TV host, "I'm expecting this black militant with an afro this big [gestures], an African dashiki on, with bones around his neck and a button on that says 'I hate honkies' and 'Death to crackers.'" But what he saw was a well-groomed man in a suit and tie, carrying a Bible.

Watts put out his hand, and the confused Clary took it, only to withdraw it quickly after the first touch. He had just broken a cardinal Klan rule. The reverend saw Clary looking at his hand and reassured him, "Don't worry, Johnny. It won't come off."

Clary started calling him a string of epithets.

"I just want to tell you I love you, and Jesus loves you," Watts replied.

The on-air back and forth featured Clary spouting off about how the races should not interact, while the reverend calmly quoted scriptural phrases. Clary was reduced to mumbling generic Klan slogans.

"I'm not listening to any more," Clary snarled, storming out.

Holding a baby in his arms, the reverend approached the Grand Dragon, who was hurriedly gathering up his belongings in the lobby. Wade introduced his fourteenth child, an adopted baby girl, born to a young white girl and black teenage boy.

"Mr. Clary, this is my daughter, Tia." As he held out the little girl with shining black eyes and skin, showering Johnny Lee with a sweet smile, Watts said, "You say you hate all black people. Just tell me," he continued, "how can you hate this child?"

The Grand Dragon nearly ran for the door. Watt's final words rang out like church bells: "God bless you, Johnny. You can't do enough to me to make me hate you. I'm gonna love you, and I'm gonna pray for you, whether you like it or not."

The embarrassment caused Clary to turn up the heat on Wade. Intimidating phone calls, crosses burning at his home and garbage strewn in his front yard failed to curb Watts's public quest for equality.

The reverend joined up with politicians to outlaw the Klan's racist telemarketing hot lines that recruited for the Klan: "Save the land, join the Klan." Johnny Lee was incensed.

Sporting KKK T-shirts, thirty Klansmen led by Clary followed Watts into a McAlester lunch spot. Surrounding him and his plate of fried chicken, Clary chortled, "Hey, boy, I'm gonna make you a promise. We are going to do the same thing to you that you do to that chicken."

Watts surveyed the Klan before picking up a piece of chicken and kissing it. The room erupted with laughter, but Clary was livid.

Clary's robed friends set fire to Watt's Jerusalem Baptist Church. The fire was extinguished before the building was totally destroyed, but Clary felt like gloating, so he called Wade, using a disguised voice. Watts greeted him cordially, saying, "Well, hello Johnny." He continued, "A man like you takes the time to call me. Let me do something for you." He begins to pray, "Dear Lord, please, forgive Johnny for being so stupid." Before hanging up, he invited Clary and his robed friends to dinner at Pete's Place in Krebs.

The Klan decided to leave him alone.

FOR MORE THAN A DECADE, Clary lived in Tulsa near Seventy-first and Lewis. He was a drinker, a fighter and a womanizer, yet he never forgot the image of little Tia, and he never forgot the impact of his grandma in Del City, praying constantly for him to quit the Klan and find the Lord. He admired Jimmy Swaggart and would smoke cigarettes while listening to Brother Swaggart go on and on about forgiveness. And Tia, who was the illegitimate daughter of a teenage J.C. Watts, a future United States representative, sneaked into his consciousness regularly.

In 1989, Johnny Lee had reached his Klan goal. He became the Imperial Wizard of the White Knights of the Ku Klux Klan, the hate and white supremacy leaders of the world. Yet, there were serious divisions within the Klan. The feds trailed his every move, and his girlfriend was unveiled as an FBI informant. At a hastily called meeting, Klan members pulled guns on Clary, claiming he was untrustworthy. Clary pointed his gun at them and backed out of the room.

The Klan was not the family he thought it might be; rather, it was full of internal hate and mistrust. Like his father before him, Clary picked up his gun, intending to end his life. A ray of sun shone through the blinds of his south Tulsa apartment and onto his Bible. Setting his gun down, he opened the holy book and read for hours.

Imperial Wizard Johnny Lee Clary quit the Klan after six months of failure. His effort to unite all the hate groups—the Skinheads, the neo-Nazis and the Aryan Nation—as a common entity ended in FBI phone tapping, arrests and brothers of hate turning on one another. He burned his robe in the backyard, feeling that "1,000 pounds" had been removed from his shoulders. He joined Billy Joe Daugherty's Victory Christian Church across from Oral Roberts University and steadfastly immersed himself in Christian education. After two years, he called Reverend Watts.

Clary told him that he had a calling to preach, and Watts invited him to give his first sermon at his rebuilt church. Half of the congregation boycotted his service. When Johnny Lee made the altar call for anyone wanting to turn their life over to Jesus, a fourteen-year-old black girl came running down the aisle, and more followed. As Johnny and the young girl passed Reverend Watts, there were tears staining the elder's face.

"Johnny, you are leading Tia to the Lord," Wade whispered. Three other Watts children joined them at the altar. The former Imperial Wizard brought the last of Watts's fourteen children into the house of the Lord.

Former Grand Wizard of the Ku Klux Klan and Tulsa resident Johnny Lee Clary became an ordained minister and works with Jimmy Swaggart, pictured here. *Johnny Lee Clary photo.*

Watts and Clary became evangelical preachers who drove across the country together. Driving through Arkansas, Clary turned to Watts and asked if he ever thought the two of them would be driving in the same car on their way to save some souls. Wade looked at him and quipped quickly, "I figured if we were ever in the same car together, you would have me in the trunk." But their relationship was on borrowed time.

Reverend Wade Watts passed in 1998. He is buried in McIntosh County, Oklahoma, beneath his tombstone that reads, "I'd give up silver and gold to have it said that I helped someone."

The Reverend Johnny Lee Clary is with the World Evangelism Fellowship and preaches for the Jimmy and Donnie Swaggart Ministries in Baton Rouge, Louisiana, where he often reminds his international TV audience that Wade Watts preached, "If you want to make beautiful music, you got to use those black and white keys together."

In the end, they enjoyed seven good years of harmony.

Chapter 4

JOE SHEETS

The Man in the Box

C all it a death parade.

A white-draped car floated quietly down the warm streets of Copan, Oklahoma. Inside the vehicle, a man held a fiery cross. Behind the car marched fifteen white-robed members of the Ku Klux Klan, their presence sending a clear message—a message that appeared on signs declaring "America for Americans." Upon reaching the Copan Undertaking Parlor, the column of Kluxers silently entered the front door of the establishment.

A flowery aroma filled the parlor where the dead man lay, his casket surrounded with arrangements from his Masonic affiliations, the Copan High School and many others. The eye-catching centerpiece was a large floral pillow sent by his brethren of the Invisible Empire, the KKK, which boasted twenty thousand members in Oklahoma at the time.

The Klan had a habit of interrupting ordinary affairs; intrusion was its modus operandi. Although the funeral service for Sheets was already underway, the hooded mourners "filed by the coffin, silently dropping a red rose on the heap of floral offerings," according to a newspaper account. Joseph C. Sheets belonged to the De Molay, the Scottish Rite and the Masonic Temple, and he had the flowers to prove it. In small towns, however, being a Mason often implied a connection to the Klan. If Sheets was ever a secret member of the Klan, his cover was blown by the large arrangement placed before his casket—a white floral pillow with red roses spelling out KKK.

The September 5, 1922 edition of the *Tulsa Daily World* noted that the Masonic Rose Croix service for Joe C. Sheets was "probably the most

The author tracked down the "man in the box" through wording on several flower sprays and the KKK rose pillow. *Danney Goble, PhD,* Tulsa! Biography of the American City.

impressive funeral ceremony ever held in Copan." Over 1,500 Masons and friends gathered at Sheets's stately home. The story left out the bit about the parade.

Sheets got his first job in oil and gas at the age of sixteen. During his career, he established himself as one of the shrewdest oil operators in the state. He was involved in management positions with the Swastika Oil and Gas Company, the Alamo Oil Company, the Collis and Jackson Oil companies and Georgia Oil and Gas Company.

In 1902, at age twenty-six, Sheets moved from his native West Virginia to Independence, Kansas, and then on to Bartlesville. He, along with his brother Earl, formed Sheets Brothers Oil and Gas. By 1905, Sheets was successful enough to move his family into a newly constructed Copan home. The prodigious structure stood out above the tent city along the railroad tracks.

Riding on the find of the Copan Oil Field discovery of 1907, the Sheets family had three hundred oil and gas wells in production within a

Right: Joe Sheets lived just north of Tulsa in the small town of Copan, Oklahoma. *Bartlesville Area History Museum.*

Below: Joe Sheets and his brother ran the oil field business from this building directly behind Joe's house. *Author collection.*

decade. A year earlier, Sheets had donated ten acres for the establishment of the Copan School District. A standalone arch structure was located at the entrance. It was called the Copan Unkwa Arch in homage to the Cherokee word for "red man."

The booming town of Copan featured four hotels to house oil laborers, a pool hall, a lumberyard and a grocery store where fights tended to break out. As a longtime member of the Copan School District Board and devoted husband to Millicent and father to Alice, Sheets served his community and family but shied away from political office, though he did serve on the Washington County Council of Defense. The Kleagles, the Klan's recruiting unit, aggressively pursued the leaders of Oklahoma wartime councils.

In addition to black gold, he had interests in farm and timber tracts and owned an insurance agency for the Northern Assurance Company Limited of London, specializing in coverage for fire, tornado, automobiles and sprinkler leakage. His local influence grew with his holdings.

The Bank of Copan opened its doors in 1910, and by 1915, Sheets was its president and principal stockholder. But all work and no play makes a dull good ol' boy, so for fun, Sheets joined the Copan Red Cross baseball team and participated in Copan wild game suppers, where the men would hunt for anything moving, large or small, even crows. The animals were cooked together in large iron kettles set up on Main Street as cheering

The photo identifies two of the players of the Red Cross baseball team. The man in the back row second from the right is Joe Sheets. *Bartlesville Area History Museum.*

This rare photo shows the Joe and Millicent Sheets house in older days. The old Sheets residence in Copan is still in great shape due to restoration by Mr. and Mrs. Dean Price. *Dean Price.*

spectators watched wrestling matches conducted in the mudhole in the center of the street.

Given the secrecy of the Klan, Sheets's exact position was not known. There was no evidence of him participating in the Klan whipping teams that flogged residents who, in the Klan's opinion, were immoral. Some whippings were exercised on prisoners turned over by local law enforcement.

Ninety-year-old Perlie Moreland knew the Sheets family well. Her parents arrived via covered wagon in Copan in 1905. Ultimately moving next door to the Sheets, she became fast friends with Millicent and Alice after Joe passed.

"Mr. Sheets was involved with the Klan—always heard about that," she comments.

She eased out of the overstuffed chair in her family room to retrieve a three-ring notebook brimming with clips and photos from the now-defunct *Copan Leader* newspaper. Plastic sleeves protect the dogged and yellowed pages with their bold-faced headlines and grainy images. Perlie has turned the screen of an old television set into a pasteboard for Scotch-taped photos of her grandchildren and great-grandchildren. Atop the old TV, a new flat-screen model balances.

Returning to her favorite chair, struggling with hip pain, Perlie settles in and opens the binder, the cover of which displays a photo of the former Bank of Copan, now a knitting supply store. Putting on her plastic framed glasses she needs only for reading, she begins turning the proud pages. A self-described "old, white-haired gal, getting shorter all the time," Perlie spins stories of Copan and Joe Sheets, who kept a Klan robe in a remote closet. Yet the Copan that Joe knew had changed.

Perlie catalogues old buildings with her camera to save at least their memories for posterity. The structures—neglected and disfigured, like an old town dog—succumb with regularity. Perlie's portraits reflect a Copan out of time. Two joints—Jessie's Café and the Truck Stop, Perlie's personal favorite—were not part of the eatery scene during the town's heyday. The vanishing memories and the new arrivals add up to a kind of empty.

Perlie acknowledges that the Klan was active in the Copan area during her youth. She'd always heard that Joe Sheets was involved in the organization, in some way. She spent hours with his widow, who knitted incessantly and loved to reminisce. According to Perlie, "Millicent had a hard time talking about it." She let all of her husband rest in peace.

Chapter 5

DIAMOND IN THE ROUGH

The 1921 Tulsa Race Riot Scapegoat

S ecreted out the alley door of the Tulsa County Jail into an awaiting car provided by Sheriff McCollough, Diamond Dick Roland took in the smoldering morning air, while thirty square blocks of Tulsa's Greenwood District burned to the ground. It was June 1, 1921, and Roland was bound for a suspect destination in Kansas City intended to keep him safe from a vigilante lynch mob. He hid in the backseat. Then, he disappeared forever.

In his absence days later, Roland was represented pro bono by court appointed attorney Wash Hudson, who was a member of Tulsa's Ku Klux Klan. Roland was formally charged by a grand jury with intent to rape a seventeen-year-old white woman named Sarah Page. Newspapers and many following historical accounts suggest that Roland's arrest triggered the Tulsa race riot of 1921. The perfumed and dapper Mr. Hudson ventured into the charred remains of Greenwood to advise Dick's mother, Damie Roland Jones, of the situation.

Damie lived in a tent provided by the Tulsa Chamber of Commerce, pitched where her family's boardinghouse and Roland's home once stood at 505 East Archer in Downtown Tulsa. (Today, it's a concession stand and centerfield entrance to the Driller baseball park.) Several months before her death in 1972, the eighty-seven-year-old survivor told interviewer Ruth Avery that she saw Dick one more time following his disappearance. There are no certifiable accounts of him returning to Tulsa. Damie claimed he had gained weight from the jail food and had the stench of a man who had

As race riot detainees march into the convention center, a corpse of a murdered black man passes by on a truck bed. *Beryl Ford Collection/Rotary Club and Tulsa Historical Society.*

hitched a ride in a train car. She said he cried to her, "Look what I have done," and left before an autumn dawn to avoid detection by angry survivors of the riot.

Roland was rumored to have moved north. Possibly working at Unity Bindery and living in an industrial neighborhood just east of downtown, a "Richard Roland" vanished from the Kansas City, Missouri public records in 1926. Damie stated Dick wrote that Page was still "bumming around Kansas City," suggesting that Roland not only knew Sarah Page but also that they were familiar. There is no census or directory information stating that Page actually lived in the metropolis. The Great Depression was on the horizon, and work was drying up. Damie says that Roland wrote of an interest to see the shores of Oregon, seeking employment in the shipyards.

A "Richard Rowland" appeared in the Portland directory in that time period, working in a mattress factory. Living in the black community of Albina, a segregated community on the outskirts of downtown, Rowland felt the full force of the Jim Crow environment so prevalent in Oregon. "Sundown laws" made it illegal for blacks to be in Portland after sundown, so they formed their own community, now known as the Albina District of Portland. Later census data proved that this Richard Rowland was a white man. Yet thousands of nameless blacks lived along the Columbia River, supporting the shipbuilding industry.

Shipbuilding outside Portland was a huge industry in the 1920s and '30s. The Henry Kaiser Shipyards expanded in anticipation of World War II needs and conducted nationwide advertisements for jobs. Around 100,000 people flocked to Oregon—many of them blacks. Kaiser built an entire community, including a housing development, schools and a hospital for six thousand of his black workers who were not wanted in Portland, calling it Vanport. On Memorial Day 1948, the Columbia River swelled fifteen feet above flood level, wiping out the complex. Lives were lost, swallowed up by the torrents. Maybe Rowland was among the nameless swept toward the Pacific.

The only Richard Rowland on the Oregon death rolls turned out to be a six-year-old boy, who lived his life in the Fairview Home (formerly the Oregon State Institute for Feeble Minded), died a tragic death and was buried in a state cemetery in Marion County, south of Portland. Evidence has since surfaced that places another Richard Rowland closer to Tulsa.

He may be resting in an all-black cemetery in Topeka, Kansas. Enforced segregation caused the creation of Mount Auburn Cemetery, which was also the burial ground for impoverished whites. Black veterans from seven different wars lie in proximity to a Richard Rowland. The records of Hall-Diffenderfer Funeral Home show him to be in the Crittenton lot. Born Richard Dean Rowland in the black Florence Crittenton Home, this child died at birth on June 3, 1936. The Dick Roland of Tulsa remained missing without a trace.

Although history books often refer to him as "Dick Rowland," the man at the center of the riot had several names. He was first called Jimmie Jones and, according to census records, became John Roland when he and Damie moved in with her parents, Dave and Ollie Roland, after 1910. Their name is misspelled as Rolland and Rowland in various census and Tulsa directories. In most news reports following the riot, Dick's last name was spelled "Rowland." According to Damie, when Jimmie entered Booker T. Washington High School, he changed his first name to Dick because he liked the name. Roland was a classmate of well-known educator W.D. Williams, who told legislator Don Ross in his publication *Impact* in June 1971 that Roland's friends called him Johnny. However, the 1921 Washington high school yearbook shows him as James Jones and J.W. Jones.

Dick Roland may be close by. In Tulsa's Oaklawn Cemetery at Eleventh and Peoria, the Roland family plot has headstones for everyone but Dick: his uncle Clarence; Clarence's daughter, Earlene Roland Morris; and grandparents Dave and Ollie, along with Damie Roland Ford and her husband, Clifford Ford. According to *Shadows of the Past: Tombstone Inscriptions*, in an adjacent section is a small headstone cryptically inscribed "James

Jones (18 years old), 1921," curiously matching Jimmy's age and the year he vanished and the year of the riot. That James Jones, however, died in March 1921, two months before Roland would've been arrested. According to the headstone located a mere ten yards from the Roland plot, James Jones was "Gone But Not Forgotten"

Post riot, the media gave him the derogatory name of Diamond Dick, stemming from the small diamond ring he wore—a birthday present given to himself from tips earned at his boot black job near the Drexel Building in Downtown Tulsa. The Drexel had a jerky elevator, where Roland once tripped, nearly fell and grabbed the arm of the operator, Sarah Page, who was by then a good and intimate friend, according to Tulsa race riot historian Eddie Faye Gates. The discomfort from Dick's hand reportedly caused the feisty, dishwater blonde to shriek and yell at Roland, which alarmed a Renberg's clothing store salesman. The salesman fabricated a wrongful tale passed onto authorities and yellow journalists.

The charge against Roland was thrown out due to District Attorney William Seaver's wrongful inclusion of assault in the charge and an alleged victim who never considered herself to be one. The demurrer of his charges in September 1921 and its signature, spelled "Dick Roland," was signed either in absentia or by the real man—no way to tell; no record of him being in Tulsa. Maybe he was already dead.

Perhaps Roland was in a "safe" jail at an undocumented location or became just another dead black man floating in the Arkansas River. Or perhaps he was placed on a flatbed truck alongside other riot corpses, or he may have been disposed of in a rural setting toward Kansas City. Maybe he was hanged in the gallows on his county jail cell floor and was carried out the alley door to his final resting place. Whatever happened to the man, when the riot started, Roland was no longer on Tulsa's mind. Maybe his mother's dementia-like ramblings to interviewer Ruth Avery were just a mother's fantasy that kept her son alive, creating a peaceful memory in her last days.

"I have lost my only boy," lamented Damie.

Could this young man be the falsely accused teenager who ignited the Tulsa race riot in 1921?

In 1921, a black young man, Dick Roland, stumbled over the threshold of an elevator, stepping on the toes of a teenage white girl. She screamed, and

Dick fled. He knew that blacks often found the end of a gallows rope following their incarceration. After his arrest, an inflammatory newspaper article suggested that he would be hanged that night, prompting a group of Greenwood black men to assemble outside the county jail to protect him from a lynch mob.

Once the riot began, all Tulsans, black and white, forgot about Dick Roland. His whereabouts after the riot were unknown and undocumented.

Many have tried to solve the mystery, looking for the 1921 yearbook of Booker T. Washington High School in Tulsa. There was a chance of a photo of Dick in the yearbook—a picture no one had ever seen. Mysteriously, two copies of the yearbook materialized at the Rudisill Library and Booker T. Washington High School. Tipped off by friend Pauline Harris of their existence, I hurried to check it out.

A rare 1921 Booker T. Washington High School Yearbook shows a "James Jones," the birthright name of a teenager perhaps also known as Dick Roland. *Author collection.*

A "Sophomore A" class photo lists a James Jones, whose class comment was, "I can't help it because I am tall." A J.W. Jones appears in the football and basketball team photos. It is the same young man.

Damie Roland Jones states that Dick Roland was her adopted son whose name was really Jimmie Jones. Out of respect for his grandparents Dave and Ollie Roland, with whom they lived, he changed his name to Roland. He chose Dick as a first name because he liked it.

W.D. Williams attended Booker T. Washington with Roland and told an interviewer that he went by "Johnny." Williams appears as a junior in the discovered yearbook and Jones as a sophomore. Williams confirmed the notion that Roland dropped out and became a shoeshine.

What can be said is that Dick/Johnny Roland and James Jones shared names, ages and schools. A direct link to the two cannot be claimed

Above: The tallest man on the team is listed as J.W. Jones. *Author collection.*

Right: Front and center in the first row of the 1921 Booker T. Washington yearbook is a J.W. Jones, likely known as Dick Roland to many in the community. *Author collection.*

unequivocally. The 1920 census shows a John Roland living with Dave and Ollie Roland. There was no James, Jimmie or J.W. Jones in the 1920 Tulsa census, which lends some credence to the two being the same person. There is no evidence to suggest they are not. Pending more definitive evidence, Dick Roland remains an enigma.

Chapter 6

TRACKING DOWN DIAMOND DICK

John Hope Franklin Reconciliation Symposium Speech on May 31, 2013

There wasn't much racial tension in my northwestern Iowa upbringing—maybe a skirmish between a few Angus and Herefords from time to time, but nothing to make front-page news. Blacks, whites and Native Americans coexisted without life-threatening prejudice.

As a child of the 1960s and '70s, I became aware of hideous acts of racial violence. I saw plenty of good people battered, bloodied and killed in what some might call acts of genocide. It made me aware that there were innocent people traumatized directly and indirectly due to extreme racial intolerance.

As a transplant to Tulsa, several decades ago, I had no idea of the racial history of Tulsa. Researching for *This Land* articles, I discovered the awful truth surrounding Memorial Day 1921. As a white man, I was appalled by the atrocities. As a member of humanity, I was enraged.

A nonevent ignited the massacre—a trumped-up allegation involving a black teenager, Dick Roland, tripping on an elevator threshold of the Drexel Building, stepping on a white girl's foot, that lead to a false claim, yellow journalism of the vilest shade and carnage in the streets above the railroad tracks, decimating the proud people and prosperous Greenwood section known as Black Wall Street.

Within days of the riot's ashes cooling, Dick was indicted by a grand jury for intent to rape, without the support of the victim, and upgraded to assault with the intent to rape by the stroke of a pen from Klansman and county attorney William Seaver. The case was thrown out three months later. There was no evidence that Dick Roland was present for any of it. He had disappeared.

Who was this Dick Roland? Where was Dick after the riot? What did he do for the rest of his life? Was there a rest of his life? It bugged me. My inner concerns for his unjustified mantle of riot perpetrator pushed me to find out more. I became obsessed with the mission to solve the mystery of the man at the center of the Tulsa race riot of 1921.

According to an account by his mother, Dick became a full-time boot black in the spring of 1921 along with a younger schoolmate, Robert Fairchild, at the Ingersoll Recreational Parlor at Third and Main, just a few long strides from the Drexel Building, where a bathroom for blacks was located on the top floor—up the elevator. Dick was a handsome, five-foot-ten young man whose jovial personality netted large tips from his oilmen customers, enough to buy a small diamond ring as a birthday gift to himself. The same ring gave the media the pseudonym of "Diamond Dick" when referencing his alleged sexual crime.

After Dick's arrest, he was moved from the city jail to the "safer" Tulsa County Jail at Sixth and Boulder. Police escorted Dick through the alley door into the basement, booked him and transported him to the top floor by elevator. Dick was along with County Sheriff McCullough, a Tulsa Klansman, and six deputies on that cellblock. McCullough turned off the elevator, leaving a narrow stairway as the only ingress-egress pathway. Prominently displayed in front of the cells was a temporary but functional gallows. For their amusement, guards occasionally tripped the trap door, causing a ricocheting bang along the concrete floors, startling and intimidating inmates.

Sheriff McCullough told Dick's mother, Damie, when he visited her at the burned-out shell of her former home, now the centerfield gate for the Tulsa Double-A baseball park, that he had taken Dick on the day of the riot to Kansas City, Kansas, to stay with some of Sarah Page's friends. Really? When testifying before the governor's post-riot commission, Sheriff McCullough claimed he slept through the night and did not hear people knocking on the cellblock door asking him to co-sign for the Oklahoma Guard to be deployed until near dawn and that he found out about the riot activity from the morning paper.

What if Dick were in Kansas City? Was it Kansas City, Kansas, or Missouri? Did he live by his given name of Jimmie Jones or Dick Roland, the last name he chose to honor his grandparents and a first name he just liked?

Working with the curator of the Kansas City, Missouri Public Library and the Wyandotte County Historical Society, outside of Kansas City, Kansas; hiring a local investigator; and personally digging for Roland or

Page information, both curators, the hired investigator and I located several possible Richard Rowland residences in the same area of Kansas City, Missouri, close to the Unit Bindery, where a Dick Rowland worked for a few years. After 1926, that Rowland vanished from Kansas City, Missouri public records. No one found evidence of a Rowland/Roland in Kansas City, Kansas.

Some say Roland and Page married in Kansas City. Yet, there are no marriage or death certificates for either, even using Richard/Dick, Rowland/Rolland/Roland and Sarah Page/Rowland. There were no hints of a Rowland or James Jones having been in Kansas City, Kansas, nor any hints of him in the nearby black town of Nicodemus.

In an interview conducted by Ruth Avery just several months before the eighty-seven-year-old Damie died, the distraught mother recounted her recollections of Dick. She claimed he would write monthly or so, once saying he heard there were good shipyard jobs in Oregon. The dates of such letters or, in fact, their existence is unknown. She told Avery that some time later, a former roommate of Dick's wrote saying Dick had died in a wharf accident—no date or location mentioned.

If Dick died on a wharf, as Damie mentioned in her only interview, there was no listing of it in Oregon state records of accidental deaths.

Scouring both Washington and Oregon, making friends with "Vinnie" of the Longshoreman's Union in Portland (and he wasn't saying nothin' to nobody), schmoozing electronically for days at a time with the good folks at the Portland and Salem Public Libraries while leaving multiple layers of finger epidermis on my keyboard, I found one Dick Rowland in Washington, who turned out to be a white man, and a Richard Rowland living in the predominantly black section of Portland, Albina, during the years 1930–37. Oregon was a strong sundowner state that demanded blacks get out of the metropolitan area by sundown, hence, the 'burb of Albina. If Dick left Kansas City for Oregon, the years 1930–37 made sense time-wise for the Rowland in Albina, even though he worked at a mattress factory rather than a wharf. Nope. No cigar. Later census details revealed that he, too, was white.

By then I had met my new best friend. She was the corresponding secretary for the Willamette Valley Genealogical Society. Her e-mails only listed her as Sue, no last name. So I dubbed her "Oregon Sue" in our e-mails and during phone conversations. She laughed. She worked hard for me.

The Kaiser Shipyards and their Vanport facility along the Columbia River just north of Portland was a good bet. Oregon Sue's mom had worked there—a "regular Rosie the Riveter," she said in an e-mail, "5' nothing and could weld in tight spaces." Henry Kaiser put out nationwide advertisements for Oregon shipyard jobs attracting thousands of pre-Depression workers from across the country. He built a community including housing, schools and a hospital for the six thousand workers—mostly blacks who were unwanted in Portland. He named it Vanport. On Memorial Day 1948, nearly twenty-seven years to the day of the Tulsa riot, the Columbia River swelled fifteen feet and wiped out Vanport, sweeping thousands of blacks into the torrent. Maybe Dick was among the nameless lost.

What if Dick were incarcerated or institutionalized in Oregon? Oregon Sue located a Richard Rowland who died in December 1936 in a state hospital called Oregon Fairview Home. This could be him. The requested death certificate arrived several days later, showing this unfortunate Richard Rowland to be a six-year-old white male who had suffered a lifetime of epilepsy before succumbing to a cerebral hemorrhage.

During my year-plus of investigation, I spoke with authors who wrote about the Tulsa race riot—people like Fort Worth resident Tim Madigan, author of the book *The Burning*, as well as former Booker T. Washington High School history teacher and a principal in the Reconciliation Commission Eddie Faye Gates, who wrote several books, including *Riot on Greenwood*. Gates and I shared numerous, unproductive phone calls. Tulsan Scott Ellsworth, who wrote the critically acclaimed book *Death in a Promised Land* that exposed the possibility of a riot mass grave, pointed me to Paul Gardullo, curator for the National Museum of African American History for the Smithsonian Institute, who was seeking information about Dick as well, but he had nothing for me. Ellsworth alerted me to playwright Erik Ehn of Brown University, who wrote and produced a play called *Diamond Dick* about the post-riot life of Dick, who was supposedly living in Kansas City, Missouri. As it turns out, the play highlights "Willie" Williams of the Dreamland Theatre in Greenwood rather than Roland. Regrettably, the impassioned, intellectual Ehn could not give me fresh information.

Changing tactics, I launched a Sarah Page investigation in her supposed home state of Missouri. In southeast Missouri, I found a burial plot with a reasonable birth date. I found ten directory listings for Pages in the county. I called every one of them—no one knew of her. The local paper had no obituary.

A tip from *This Land* magazine that he may be in a Topeka cemetery led me down an interesting path. It seems that during the 1920s and '30s, there were separate Topeka directories for whites and blacks, but there was no listing for a Rowland. Like other cities, Topeka had black cemeteries.

I uncovered the funeral home that had buried a Richard Rowland in the mostly-black Mt. Auburn Cemetery in June 1936. The Kansas Historical Society gave me the name of a man at Hall-Diffenberger Funeral Home who was the record keeper of Dick's out-of-business burial company. After retrieving the basement file, I was told the boy died at birth at the black Florence Crittenden home.

Some things are right under your nose, so I checked. I talked with an animated and gracious Lorenzo Vann of Tulsa. He maintained that many were sure Dick and Sarah married in Kansas City, Missouri, returning to Tulsa, where Dick worked at the Mayo Hotel. The current Mayo management determined that all employee records were thrown out when the hotel closed in the 1980s.

Former Oklahoma legislator and publisher of *Impact* Don Ross did not have any pearls for me. His son, Kavin Ross, told me of a Tulsa North church, Rentie Grove Baptist Church, that might have been the Roland family church. I enlisted the help of a friend, Frances Jordan, executive director of the Greenwood Cultural Center, who went there on a Wednesday night to talk with the preacher, Mr. Green, about a possible congregational photo album, hoping for a picture of Dick and his family. When she walked in, they were having a prayer meeting. The eyes of the four ladies and the preacher lit up. Frances chortled, "They thought I was a new recruit!" She left without querying the preacher. Subsequently, Frances went to Preacher Green's house, but it was empty.

I needed to have a photo for this story—one that had never been published. I contacted the Tulsa Public Schools, which said the Archive Room was undergoing a remodel with no completion date in sight, while the boxes of yearbooks and memorabilia were stored in a remote grade school, unavailable to the general pubic. I called my good friend Dr. Pauline Harris, human rights coordinator for Tulsa Public Schools, asking if she knew of anybody who might have a 1921 BTW yearbook. She made some calls, striking out, but promised to call if she found one.

I enlisted the help of BTW assistant principal Mike Sims and met with him over a photo he found of a similarly named young man in a yearbook, but it was from the 1940s. On several trips to the high school library, I mined all the archival materials, including yearbooks. Nada. The yearbook collection started with 1922, just one year shy of the year I needed.

Out of the blue, Dr. Harris called with good news—someone had donated a 1921 BTW annual to Rudisill Library. I raced to the front desk. Without picture captions, the photos could not identify Jimmie, but, as James Jones, he did offer a quote under his sophomore class picture, saying, "I can't help it because I am tall."

Inspired, I headed for the high school library, and there was another copy of the 1921 BTW yearbook, but this one was from an online service, and it had photo captions listing a J.W. Jones in basketball and football team pictures, along with James Jones in the sophomore class picture. In that era, it was commonplace to use two initials rather than a first name. While there can be some reasonable doubt it is him, I was silently screaming, "Bingo!"

Damie stated the her son dropped out of high school several times, only returning to play sports. She recalled that during his second year of high school, he dropped out for good. That would be his sophomore year, when folks claimed the downtown shoeshiner was eighteen or so. That would be the riot year of 1921.

Further, according to the 1920 census records for all Jones families in Tulsa, there were no young men between the ages of twelve and twenty with the name of Jimmie or James or initials starting with J. So it can be argued that, within that time period, there were no known young men in Tulsa who called themselves James Jones, other than Dick Roland who used his Jones name for school registrations.

Maybe Dick or Jimmie was closer to home? I chatted with all the burial list people at all the cemeteries in Tulsa. Zero. Then I struck a vein of gold at Eleventh and Peoria. Aware that the forward-thinking Dave Roland, Damie's dad and Dick's granddad, had purchased a family plot, I found it just blocks from the Greenwood district in Oaklawn Cemetery. The plot has everyone but Dick: his Uncle Clarence, cousin Earlene and his grandparents Dave and Ollie, along with his mother, Damie Jones Ford, and her husband, Clifford.

Tulsan John Hope Franklin was awarded the Presidential Medal of Freedom in 1995, and his book *From Slavery to Freedom* has sold over three million copies. *Greenwood Cultural Center.*

The Tower of Reconciliation in the center of John Hope Franklin Park stands tall against the backdrop of downtown Tulsa. *Author collection.*

According to *Shadows of the Past: Tombstone Inscription*, in an adjacent section is a small headstone cryptically inscribed "James Jones (18 years old), 1921," curiously matching Jimmie's age and the year he vanished and the year of the riot. The grave marker for that James Jones, however, shows he died in March 1921, two months before Roland would have been arrested. According to the headstone located a mere ten yards from the Roland plot, James Jones was "Gone But Not Forgotten."

The author presented this speech to the John Hope Franklin Symposium on May 31, 2013. Dr. John Hope Franklin was the son of Buck Franklin, whose legal representation of black Greenwood residents after the race riot was key to them retaining their real estate and other concerns. Dr. John Franklin was one of the leading black historians and activists in American history.

Chapter 7

FIRST CHARGED, LAST FREED

The Exonerated Czar of Greenwood

John the Baptist moved to Tulsa in 1899. The Stradford family called him J.B. He was a former Kentucky slave who was not afraid to preach the gospel of equal treatment and racial solidarity for black Americans. College-educated in Ohio at Oberlin College, Stradford received his law degree from Indiana University, practicing in Indianapolis and yearning to influence black equality. Tulsa became his destiny. Leaders of the local white community yearned for his demise.

In America, the late 1800s provided an unpainted canvas of opportunity for post-emancipation blacks. They were free to relocate, joining up with other freshly freed blacks and freedmen from Creek native enslavement to start communities separate from the white population. While racial distrust remained, their new beginnings were sites of burgeoning entrepreneurship.

Over 60 percent of the U.S. black population served whites as domestics, restaurant cooks, bootblacks and laborers. Wages were brought back to their new settlements and spent with black grocers, black lumberyards, black saloons and gambling enterprises, black theaters and a cadre of like-skinned businesses.

Oklahoma's future looked bright for blacks. Led by the vision of Edwin McCabe, founder of the first black community of Langston in 1890, the state became a mecca for black towns and self-reliant communities—fifty by 1920. The *New York Times* warned on March 1, 1890, that a Negro settlement is a camp of savages. McCabe sent recruiters to the South, appealing to racial pride, and hoped to recruit enough blacks to become the majority race, forcing the whites to turn over the region to them.

McCabe's dream of a politically powerful, black-friendly state lured Stradford from Indianapolis to the dirt streets of Tulsa's undeveloped Greenwood area.

Buying up large tracts of undeveloped land northeast of the tracks that bordered downtown, thirty-nine-year-old J.B. Stradford sold his Greenwood parcels to blacks only. O.W. Gurley, the acknowledged founder of the new community, did the same as Black Tulsa took shape.

Yet Stradford was not a real estate man by trade. He was a University of Indiana–educated attorney, who used his investment profits to aggressively litigate for black social justice. Never shy to voice his outrage, he occasionally declared, "The day a member of our group was mobbed (lynched) in Tulsa, the streets would be bathed in blood." The activist put himself on the line to prevent lynchings. In 1918, he turned back a lynching mob in Bristow, Oklahoma. When Stradford suffered Jim Crow discrimination, he did not sit idly.

Walking along Greenwood Avenue, a white deliveryman made a racist remark about Stradford's skin color. Nearly beating him to death, Stradford had to be pulled by friends off the bloodied iceman, and they told him that if he killed the white man, he would be mobbed, a euphemism for lynched. Later, he was acquitted for violating Oklahoma Jim Crow laws.

Riding a train from Kansas to Tulsa in 1912, nearly fifty years after the end of the Civil War, J.B. experienced the continuation of slave law in Oklahoma. When the locomotive reached the Oklahoma border, the conductor stopped the train, and Stradford was forcibly removed from the black luxury car, although he had paid the higher fare. Oklahoma exempted railroads from the expense of such cars if it did not make economic sense. Stradford sued Midland Valley Railroad in state and federal courts for false imprisonment. All courts ruled against his demand for justice by law, angering Greenwood residents.

In 1916, Stradford railed the Tulsa City Commission for its segregation ordinance that he claimed casted "a stigma upon the colored race in the eyes of the world; and to sap the spirit of hope for justice before the law from the race itself." The upside of segregation was that the "white" dollars earned by black Tulsans stayed in the district, giving Deep Greenwood merchants the spoils of their neighbors, while the black print media continued to pull no punches.

The most militant black voice in America and a founder of the NAACP fanned the embers during a Greenwood speech. Brought to the community by Stradford and newspaperman A.J. Smitherman in March 1921, the first black Harvard PhD. W.E.B. Du Bois lectured the throngs that the hatred in the white man's heart was still strong. At times, the professor proposed that the only solution to hate is hate.

Du Bois argued in those times, "We have suffered and cowered. When the armed lynchers come, we too must gather armed. When the mob moves, we propose to meet it with sticks and clubs and guns." There was a rising tide of passion in Greenwood. Residents were ready to forcefully defend the promise of equality under the law.

White Tulsa became less enchanted with the likes of J.B. Stradford. Although Stradford was respected as a legitimate businessman, many Tulsans despised him.

Stradford and his close friend Andrew J. Smitherman, the owner/publisher of the black newspaper *Tulsa Star* situated on Greenwood Avenue, spoke out against the trio of leading causes of civil rights in Oklahoma—lynching, voting rights and the railroad segregation policy. Smitherman's counterpart in Oklahoma City, the *Black Dispatch*, a black Oklahoma City newspaper published by Roscoe Dunjee, paralleled *Tulsa Star* concerns. Dunjee regularly fired up blacks in the Greenwood district, declaring that Oklahoma's courts were full of dead lynched men's bones, denied enforcement of the United States Supreme Court decision that validated black Oklahoman's right to vote and supported Oklahoma's railroad segregation statute that created separate railcars for whites and blacks. During vaudeville shows at the famed Dreamland Theatre in Deep Greenwood, a frequently bantered slogan was "Don't let the white man run it over on you, but fight." Racial rhetoric primed Tulsa.

While inflammatory verbiage continued in district tabloids and on street corners, business was good. J.B. Stradford amassed a sizeable bank account. With fifteen rental houses, including a sixteen-room brick apartment building, he earned a real estate income of nearly $8,000 a month in 2013 dollars.

Stradford decided it was time that black travelers of means should have accommodations as swank as downtown's Hotel Tulsa. He envisioned his hotel as the pinnacle of his dreams, remarking, "The Stradford would be a monument to the thrift, energy and business tact of the race in Tulsa [and] to the race in the state of Oklahoma." The exuberant opening of his eponymous hotel on June 1, 1918, signified the realization of his promised land, adding credence to Booker T. Washington's description of this district as Black Wall Street.

The three-story edifice of pressed brick above the windows and stone slabs below cost a glitzy $50,000. The segregated Stradford, serving blacks

The Stradford Hotel located in Greenwood was the most successful black-owned, black-only hotel in America. *Greenwood Cultural Center.*

only, was the largest black-owned and -operated hotel in America. While it fulfilled his dream, the construction of the hotel created financial difficulties. Stradford ran out of money. Borrowing $20,000 helped, yet when a boxcar of beds, rugs and chandeliers rolled into the station, the new hotelier could not pay the $5,000 bill.

Within eyeshot of the hotel, the furnishings for the fifty-four modern "living rooms," gambling hall, dining hall and saloon languished on the rails. Stradford negotiated paying a quarter of the total and the remainder in monthly payments. The Stradford Hotel at 301 North Greenwood was open for business.

It was a gay time. A new form of music ricocheted up Greenwood Avenue from the dancehalls like the Commodore Cotton Club. Jazz, with its gyrating rhythms and freedom to improvise, stimulated the dancers and frightened the white community, which considered the music style as vibrations for the half-savage. The piano in the Stradford Hotel pounded out jazz for its distinguished clientele, who tripped the fantastic toe.

Amid the glamor of the Stradford, the racial tension in Greenwood and the region was superficially suppressed. Desperate events stoked emotions.

Greenwood celebrated the success of a group of Muskogee black men who, in mid-April 1921, stormed the city jail, liberated a black man (John

McShane) and shot a white deputy sheriff in the process. The local black community justified the action, claiming they had prevented a lynching. Their defiance energized Greenwood.

Stradford and Smitherman agreed that a community must be vigilant if a black man was in danger of being lynched. It was justice—a legal right, they reckoned, to take aggressive action, encouraging their community to support armed militancy toward lynching.

In the May 30, 1921 afternoon edition of the *Tulsa Tribune*, a front-page story announced that a "negro will be lynched tonight." The following day, Greenwood teenager Dick Roland was arrested under the allegations that he had attempted to rape a seventeen-year-old white girl, Sarah Page, in an elevator. Although a grand jury indictment against him was rendered several days later and then dismissed within three months for lack of a prosecution witness (Sarah, according to oral histories from Greenwood survivors, was actually his taboo lover) and a District Attorney's tampering with the charges, the yellow-journalism article fomented the deadliest and most destructive "riot" in the history of the United States—an event that would forever be referred to as the Tulsa race riot of 1921.

The *Tulsa Star* office in Deep Greenwood was the center of activity the night before the battle. Several carloads of passionate armed veterans made repeated trips from the newspaper's curb to the jail holding Roland, where they confronted a growing white mob. Dedicated to stopping a lynching, J.B. held court with the gathering crowd, repeating his oft-used statement about "blood in the streets." He recalled in his memoirs that he declared to the nervous onlookers what he would do if there were a lynching: "If I can't get anyone to go with me, I will go single-handed and empty my automatic into the mob and, then, resign myself to my fate," he roared. His comments encouraged men, including a tall, light-skinned veteran named O.B. Mann, to continue making trips to the courthouse.

Mann, a successful Greenwood grocer, returned from the war with inflated ideas about equality and sure he could take on the world, according to O.W. Gurley during court testimony on an insurance claim relating to property damage from the riot. Gurley maintained that it was the inadvertent discharge of Mann's handgun when grabbed by a white man that activated the fatal chain of events.

At dawn, the sound of an air horn commanded the heavily armed white armada, loaded with Klansmen, to step over the tracks, attacking an underarmed band of black veterans in uniform and frightened Greenwood residents intent on defending their families and homes.

Within a matter of hours, hundreds were murdered. Homes and businesses were looted and burned as thousands of black Tulsans were arrested and herded into detention.

Dick Roland was a forgotten man. Sheriff McCollough claims Dick spent a safe evening in the county jail and was secreted out of town by 8:00 a.m. the next morning amid the gunfire of the massacre, never, according to most, to return to Tulsa. The carnage would continue through the day.

The June 1, 1921 evening edition of the *Tulsa Tribune* wrote, "A motley procession of negroes wended its way down Main Street to the baseball park with hands held high above their heads, their hats in one hand, a token of their submission to the white man's authority." The reporter continued, "They will return, not to their homes, but to heaps of ashes, the angry reprisal for the wrong inflicted on him by the inferior race." Some of that race under siege resisted the roundup.

Attempting to hold the mobsters from advancing, Stradford and others fired from the second-story porch that fronted the hotel. The building represented black equality to him, and he preferred death over losing it. The west-facing windows on the third floor had been shattered by bursts of lead from a machine gun. Six men were wounded, and one was dead.

The hotel became a haven for black families. Most left, surrendering to the militia. A sobbing Augusta, Stradford's wife, pleaded with him, "Oh, papa, let us go, too!"

"If you want to go with the crowd, then go," he said. "I intend to protect my hotel."

Augusta stayed. Others returned with a message of hope. The militia had promised to keep the hotel from further destruction, if Stradford surrendered. He agreed.

A short, slightly rotund man with a pencil-thin mustache perched above his squared chin, the now sixty-year-old Stradford was reportedly the wealthiest man in Greenwood, with over $1.6 million dollars of investments in today's currency. He stood with his gun in the doorway of his hotel, waiting for the car of his captors. His dark, piercing eyes surveyed the burning buildings in Deep Greenwood. Hundreds of the eight thousand Greenwood residents ran through the street before him. Some with raised hands were marshaled to detention centers, with shots fired at their feet and hopelessness on their faces.

A man described by descendants as having the strength of a Mandingo warrior, Stradford watched mobsters enter his building. They took him to the convention center, where city officials took $2,000 of his money from his

J.B. Stradford was marched into Tulsa's convention center like thousands of members of his black community. *Beryl Ford Collection/Rotary Club and Tulsa Historical Society.*

pockets. There is no mention of Augusta's whereabouts. Stradford was not detained long, but he was still in harm's way.

One day later, an order asked for the arrest of Stradford so he could face a grand jury. The contention was that he had encouraged carloads of armed blacks who organized and left from the Stradford Hotel.

Without his presence, on June 6, J.B. Stradford became the first person formally charged with inciting a riot. To be proven guilty, the county district attorney only needed to show he abetted the riot that resulted in murder, looting and theft—never mind that those crimes were committed by the white mob. The penalty for the charge was death or life imprisonment. The white community needed a definable villain, and it decided on Stradford.

His name was well known in the Tulsa white community. His railroad segregation lawsuit as well as his defiance toward the segregation ordinance put him squarely in opposition to the community members' values. He named a hotel after himself, so they knew he was a man of ambition. As Greenwood's Republican Party leader, the local papers named him a "henchman." Since the media labeled the riot a "Negro uprising," they reasoned that the wealthiest, most defiant and outspoken man must be the ringleader—and he fled, so he must be guilty.

With authorities on his heels, Stradford leaned back in a segregated railroad car headed for Independence, Kansas. Through a gentle rain,

Stradford gazed up Greenwood Avenue, spying his symbol of black pride reduced to smoldering ashes and charred brick. Oklahoma was no longer the Promised Land.

Along with hundreds of black Americans who died on June 1, 1921, and thousands who had homes, businesses and possessions stolen or burned, the Stradford Hotel laid in ruins, never to be reconstructed. The crown jewel of Black Tulsa shined a scant three years to the day.

Shortly after arriving at his brother's house in Independence, local police, at the request of Tulsa authorities, paid a visit to Stradford. Asked if he would turn himself in, he replied, "Hell, no." Arrested and booked, he called his son in Chicago. Cornelius Stradford, a graduate of Columbia University Law School, took the first train to Kansas and posted the $6,500 (2013 value) bond. J.B. was told to stay put and appear in court on June 10. Convinced he would not get a fair trial if returned to Tulsa, Stradford and his son boarded the next train to Chicago. Incensed, Tulsa litigators vowed to extradite and try him for the charge of inciting a riot.

Wrangling successfully against the extradition attempts, the aging Stradford settled into Chicago life with his wife, son and numerous grandchildren. Trying to re-create his success in Tulsa, he practiced law and filed a suit in September against the American Central Insurance Company for $65,000, trying to recover some of his real estate losses. Stradford did not appear at the hearing. Due to the riot exclusion clause in insurance policies and local leaders defining the travesty as a "riot," all riot victims' claims, including the one by the gentleman considered by some to be an outlaw, were knocked out in legal fights.

Desiring to re-create his real estate prowess, he formed a group of investors to build a luxury hotel like the Stradford. Regrettably, the project ran out of money and the building was not completed. He did, however, construct a candy store, barbershop and a small pool hall. His modest business holdings in Chicago reminded him of what once was.

Stradford lost more than money in the Tulsa race riot of 1921. He lost his black sense of place. In his unpublished memoirs, he wrote, "It is incredible to believe that in this civilized age that a white man could be so void of humanity." He continued, "My soul cried for revenge and prayed for the day to come when I could personally avenge the wrongs which had been perpetrated against me." He died in 1935 at the age of seventy-four. Sixty years later, family members extracted his atonement.

Cornelius E. Toole was a former NAACP lawyer and a Cook County, Illinois circuit court judge. He was also a great-grandson of J.B. Stradford.

Toole harbored resentment for the smearing of his relative's name and the destroying of his properties and his dreams. Through impassioned communications with Mayor Susan Savage and local black leader Don Ross in 1996, the sixty-three-year-old former judge insisted that the charges against Stradford be dismissed. The decision rested on the shoulders of first-year district attorney Bill LaFortune, who needed to render an opinion on a strict legal question—did evidence support the notion that Stradford incited a riot?

Nancy Little was assigned to the investigation. Her detailed inspection revealed that innocent black families suffered a ruthless attack. She was shocked. While it was undeniable that Stradford violated law by jumping bail and refusing extradition, Little concluded that he was innocent of inciting a riot. LaFortune vacated the charges.

In October 1996, Stradfords from Texas, Illinois, Ohio and New York set foot in Oklahoma for the first time since June 1921. The vindication ceremony at the Greenwood Cultural Center featured moving statements from Governor Frank Keating. Quite simply, District Attorney Bill LaFortune presented the motion to dismiss, and Judge Jesse Harris accepted it.

John the Baptist Stradford was the first riot victim indicted and the last alleged outlaw exonerated—first charged, last freed.

Part II

DIRIGIBLE FLYOVER:
ZEPPELIN CIRCLES DOWNTOWN TULSA

Chapter 8

USS *Los Angeles* Floats Over Tulsa in 1929

Crowds Watch from Rooftops

A s part of its reparation to the United States for war debt, Germany
gave the United States the ZR-3 (Zeppelin Rigid #3) airship—the
same kind of airship that was responsible for the destruction of London.
The vessel was constructed under an agreement with the British that it
would be a commercial passenger aircraft. The metal, substructured LTA

White-shirted workers rushed to the rooftops to catch a glimpse of a Zeppelin given to the
United States Navy. *Beryl Ford Collection/Rotary Club and Tulsa Historical Society.*

The USS *Los Angeles* appeared to be headed for a specially built mooring atop a building, but it circled the downtown without stopping. *Beryl Ford Collection/Rotary Club and Tulsa Historical Society.*

(Lighter Than Air) arrived at the Lakehurst Naval Air Station in New Jersey on October 15, 1924.

President Coolidge commissioned the ZR-3 dirigible as a navy vessel shortly thereafter. A dirigible is a lighter-than-air airship. Blimps are a type of dirigible with no internal structure, so they deflate when pressure escapes. Zeppelins are dirigibles with internal frames and were manufactured by Luftschiffbau Zeppelin of Germany.

"I'm going to name this new airship the *Los Angeles* because it has come to us from overseas like an angel of peace," said Navy Secretary Curtis Wilbur.

Its main purpose was to provide reconnaissance support for naval fleets. Before being decommissioned in 1932 and stored in its Lakehurst hangar, the *Los Angeles* logged over 172,000 miles and flew 331 missions. It had the distinction of being the only navy dirigible that did not crash.

The *Los Angeles* doubled as an important public relations tool, used to promote the navy's neophyte dirigible air force, when it made numerous trips to the eastern and the southern states.

Enroute from a top-off at a helium plant in Amarillo to its Lakehurst hanger, the airship charted a course through Tulsa and Chicago in 1929. The top of the Mayo Hotel in downtown Tulsa provided a close-up perspective of the massive, six-hundred-foot airship as it glided past white-shirted workers, jammed on rooftops for a bird's eye view.

The America of the late 1920s was a lively national community, blissfully unaware of a looming Great Depression. In Tulsa, oil baron Waitte Phillips was depositing an average of $25,000 a day into the Exchange National Bank at Third and Boston. In anticipation of supporting planned dirigible travel across the country, patterned after Germany's successful commercial airship trade, a network of dirigible moorings were constructed on the tallest buildings in larger cities across the country, usually banks. Such was the case with the 1928 top-out completion of the Exchange National Bank.

A second Mayo photo shows the *Los Angeles* as it nears the newly constructed Tulsa mooring. That was the closest the structure came to tethering a dirigible. If the ship had stopped in Tulsa, a bracket from the mooring to the tip of the *Los Angeles* would allow the huge vessel to rotate around the mooring according to the wind direction. Passengers would walk a gangplank from the tip to the mooring and descend into the building.

Never used for commercial passenger travel, this rigid airship frequently transported politicians, foreign bureaucrats as well as the king and queen of Siam. No telling who was aboard the *Los Angeles* on that day in 1929 when it did a forty-mile-per-hour fly-by of the Exchange National Bank mooring well below its sixty-eight-mile-per-hour maximum.

Part III

COLORFUL PERSONALITIES:
NATIVE GIANTS AND A HAMBURGER NAZI

Chapter 9

THEY MIGHT BE GIANTS

A Pigskin Bushwhack in the Osage

Having finished a midday meal on their small kitchen stoves, a group of native athletes walked from the Southern Hotel and boardinghouse off Main Street in Hominy, just north of Tulsa, to a football scrimmage on a rough patch of the Osage reservation near downtown. The warm-up was the beginning of preparation for a Christmas Day game with the newly crowned NFL champions, the New York Giants. The same practice turf served them a year prior when they trained for professional football's New York Rangers, led by Red Grange, the "Galloping Ghost." The locals lost by a touchdown at a Tulsa stadium in a game orchestrated by legendary sports promoter Sam Avey.

Typical of the era, professional football teams barnstormed the country following the regular season. Attracted by the potential to earn extra paychecks, the Giants' ultimate destination on their way through Oklahoma was the glitter of Los Angeles and a team dubbed the "Pride of the West."

Hominy became one of five authorized, north-central Oklahoma settlements for the Osage Nation when the U.S. government relocated the tribe in the early 1870s from the Diminished Reserve in Kansas. Settling along a creek they named for their tribal leader "Walks in the Night," or Ho'n-Mo'n-I'n, the uncommonly large natives, many of them exceeding six feet in height and weighing over two hundred pounds, cleared areas for agriculture.

Fewer than five hundred populated the settlement at the time of Oklahoma statehood in 1907. As the Osage developed their government

The Hamilton brothers, Otto and the seated Ira, played on an all-native football team for a small town just north of Tulsa. Ira was the founder of the team and its first coach. *Osage Tribal Museum.*

allotments, agricultural production centered on cotton, corn, hogs and cattle while supporting several stockyards. The cultural mix and the revenue source changed dramatically in 1916 with the discovery of the Hominy Oil Field, attracting more than two thousand mostly-white oil field workers and attorneys, as well as car dealerships, movie theaters, hotels and banks over the next few years.

Head right payments from oil production on Osage allotments instantly created several thousand wealthy natives by generating an average current value of $165,000 annually. A group of Osage men funded an upstart football team led by rancher Ira Hamilton. "Papa," related an enthusiastic daughter, Irene Hamilton Lazelle, in a phone call to her Hominy residence, "belonged to an American Native Church, organizing the men to get together and play football." The team began in 1923 to play teams formed by American Legions of neighboring cities in Kansas and Oklahoma. Success came quickly, yet the team lacked the resources for equipment and travel.

In 1925, four Hominy Osage men bankrolled the team. Underwritten primarily by Dick Rusk, Harry Big Eagle, Allison Webb and Ed Labelle, the backing provided uniforms and travel expenses. Team founder Hamilton relinquished his coaching duties and assumed the left guard position. Ira's brother Otto became a well-respected center, Bill Shadlow dominated the front line and the towering Pete Big Horse played right guard while fathering eight children who continue to play pivotal roles in the Osage community.

One of the Hominy Indians offered NFL experience of his own. Joe Pappio played offensive line for Jim Thorpe's Oorang Indians before moving back to Hominy. In game films stored in the Hominy town library, the padless Pappio and 240-pound Buck Harding leveled multiple defensive linemen, separating them from their leather helmets, allowing backs like Salter Fixico and John Levi to plunge for long gains. Pappio returned to the NFL for the 1930 season with the Chicago Cardinals.

Organized around the extreme talents of Prague, Oklahoma's Jim Thorpe, the NFL Oorang Indians hailed from LaRue, Pennsylvania, population under one thousand. The team owner, Walter Lingo—who purchased the franchise for $100 in 1922— believed there was a supernatural link between the Airedale dog breed and Native Americans. His passion for both led him to establish an all-Indian professional football team as a marketing tool that employed only natives as players. For $500 a week, Thorpe managed and played for the team and ran the Oorang Airedale Kennel along with his teammates—a Lingo requirement for playing time.

Thorpe, a Sac and Fox Indian with a tribal name meaning "Bright Path," piloted the touring team that played twenty games in the NFL, winning only three during their brief run in 1922–23. The team folded in 1924, and the kennels succumbed to the advent of the Great Depression in 1929. Olympic champion Thorpe never played for the Hominy Indians.

In the early years, a baseball pitcher from Guthrie carried the Indians team. His name was Johnny "Pepper" Martin. While a fixture at third base for the St. Louis Cardinals, Martin was nicknamed—in an era fond of nicknames—the "Wild Horse of the Osage." As Martin moved on to the Major Leagues, the Hominy Indians received an infusion of outside talent, among them an All-American named John "Skee" Levi, who claimed a smattering of Jewish and mostly Arapaho ancestry, played multiple sports for the Haskell Institute in Lawrence, Kansas (still there, but now called the Haskell Indian Nations University). He played for a time with the New York Yankees affiliate in Harrisburg, Pennsylvania. "Got homesick, I had to come back to my people," said Levi. Thorpe said he was the best football player he'd ever seen. He completed seventy-five-yard passes, and standing on the fifty-yard line, he could drop-kick field goals routinely.

Preparing for a post-season game in Muskogee that was to be his final game for Haskell, Levi borrowed fifty cents from a coach for a haircut prior to a visit from Fred Lookout, the son of the Osage chief. The Hominy Indians were practicing for an upcoming game with a rival town, Fairfax. The chief described a dire set of circumstances created by the "squaw men" organizers of Fairfax, mostly white cowboys and boomers who married Indian brides, who had hired the entire Kansas City Cowboys, an NFL team, to play for them.

"You've got to help us," Lookout explained. "We, full-bloods, have many thousands of dollars bet on this game," reportedly as much as $200,000 in 1925 dollars or over $2 million in current value. Additionally, he promised, if Levi and his teammates would play, the Osage would make a sizeable donation to the construction of the new Haskell football stadium. Several days later, at the end of a lavish Osage banquet held in Hominy celebrating the entire Haskell team, all agreed to play.

Billed as the "Cowboys vs. the Indians" and played on the side of a hill in neighboring Fairfax, it was said that the setting sun produced a burst of light as Levi scored the winning touchdown. After a game that did not field one Hominy or Fairfax resident, John Abbott, one of the few Osage sponsors who could speak English, declared, "We Osages mighty proud." The check written in the fall of 1925 for the stadium equated to $506,800 in current dollars.

Although no one got rich playing for the Indians, they were thrilled to get paid playing football with fellow natives. The scale for post-season games against the richer East Coast teams ranged from $25 ($300 current dollars) to $150 ($1,800). During the regular twelve-game season and for games played closer to home, they played only for a share of the gate. Then there was the betting.

The Hominy Indian football team played several games in Tulsa, beating the then World Champion New York Giants in 1927. *Osage Tribal Museum.*

"I've heard stories about some pretty high betting going on during the games," said Irene Hamilton Lazelle. Asked about the reports that some Osage would slip a player a few greenbacks when he scored or made a big play, Irene laughed sweetly and said, "Papa wouldn't have approved" of tips for touchdowns.

Attempting to attract spectators, the team often dressed in ceremonial garb before the game and performed native dances. Raymond Luttrell, brother of player-manager Homer Luttrell, tells this story about a hotel stay in New York: "Some players emerged from the elevator with fullback Fixico wrapped in a blanket, and he let out an Indian yell. It caused the old ladies to clear out and made the reporters a little hesitant to approach the players."

Richard Luttrell, son of Homer, said his father told him of the mischievous Fixico taunting the opposing defense by pointing, a la Babe Ruth, to where he would run through the line or score a touchdown. After zigzagging around the backfield with the ball and with the defense in disarray, Chief Fixico pulled it off, heading through the end zone and the fence behind it.

"Chief" was a name Fixico gave to himself. Many other players followed suit. Staying in the Hominy and the Oberlyn Hotels along with many of those coming to watch the games, the team got a "gib kick out of signing fictitious names to the register an' then watch th' easterners, who'd stop there, lookin' at the names," according to *Oologah Oozings* editor and publisher Bill Hoge in a December 1947 article. He continued, "They made up a lot wild soundin' 'injun' names."

Known as "Big Chief" according to his daughter, Jackie, Pete Lazelle was the kicker for the Hominy Indians football team and captain of the high school basketball team. *Author collection.*

One of the most daunting to wear the Indians uniform was Pete Lazelle. Lazelle graduated from Hominy High School in 1923, where he captained the basketball and football teams. At six foot six inches and more than two hundred pounds, he was called "Big Chief" according to his daughter, Jackie, who now resides in neighboring Skiatook. She said, "His father was French, and his mother was Potawatomie from Shawnee. She operated a spa-like sweathouse adjacent to the main house. The house was so close to the railroad tracks, the doors creaked and the windows shook from the rumble of the trains." Lazelle kicked extra points after touchdowns, sometimes into cow pastures.

The Hominy home field, itself a pasture, sported a metal cable that cordoned off the playing surface. Fans drove their cars right up to the cable and sat on their hoods or dragged benches and chairs to front-row positions along the barrier, recalled Irene Lazelle. The nouveau riche natives of the period had the bucks for the fancy sedans and fur coats of the spectators ringing the perimeter.

Eschewing the hayseed pasture for the concrete stands of Osage Park in nearby Pawhuska, the local American Legion organizers prepared for the Indians' showdown with the Giants. An ever-changing collection of players from eleven different native tribes, including an Eskimo, made up the Hominy Indian professional football team that was in the middle of a prodigious twenty-eight-game winning streak. An unknown sportswriter had penned them "the terrors of the Midwest."

The New York Giants pulled out of St. Louis in late December 1927, headed, ultimately, for Los Angeles on the westbound Texas Special luxury train. Stepping off the posh, KATY railroad cars just north of Tulsa and onto the brown, Pawhuska high school stadium turf, the newly crowned champions warmed up for the gridiron tussle with the local heroes.

Lacking the funds for a bus, the home team arrived in its usual caravan of Buicks and Pierce Arrows. Little Feather, Big Twig, White Eagle, Running Hawk, John Levi and their tribe of twenty entered the gates to the cheers of two thousand townies and visitors.

The *Daily Journal Capital* of Oklahoma City reported in its account of the competition that the Giants dominated the first quarter with a "brilliant passing game" and "undoubtedly would have meant a victory, if 'Dutch' Hill had played his customary flashy game." Yet his four dropped passes kept them off the scoreboard. It became their undoing when one such pass deflected off Hill into an unnamed Indians player's hands, who, stimulated by a screaming grandstand, raced fifty yards to take the early lead.

Then, fill-in Giant halfback Ben Hobson, who played for the Buffalo NFL team during the regular season, broke the scoring drought for the Giants with a bruising five-yard run off tackle in the second quarter.

Levi took over for Hominy, executing bullet-like passes, including a third-quarter, sixty-yard touchdown strike at the goal line to a stretched out Pappio.

The fourth quarter was a slugfest. The Giants flailed wildly with a series of deceptive plays, but the Indians covered them all. As the clock reached the end, the scoreboard declared the improbable results: Hominy Indians 13, New York Giants, 6.

The crowd rushed the field, and the bookies paid off bettors.

Chapter 10

NO PHONES, NO FOOLS, NO FRETS

The J.J. Behind J.J.'s Gourmet Burger Café

J.J. Conley lounges against the cushions of a private room at Lucky's. He studies his glass of Syrah and takes a sip. He is a smallish man, elegantly dressed, looking something like an aging *GQ* model. He isn't the scruffy commoner you would expect to find running a burger joint. But Conley's is not a common burger joint. For decades, it has been a curious, almost intimidating place to eat.

J.J.'s Gourmet Burger Café is a pure reflection of its owner. Loaded with bravado, rules and charm, the entire place exposes his soul. Yet J.J. would disagree with you. It is his way.

"Naïve people believe just about anything," Conley says, adding, "Good lies make good stories."

Born Jerry James Conley to a German immigrant who never quite had his adoption papers in order, J.J. had the paternally invented last name of Conley. Hansberger was his father's birth name. It was a nonissue until the FBI scrutinized him for clearance to work with sensitive information as a defense airman. A hasty call to Dad revealed the truth that Papa had hoped "would never become an issue." The feds frowned but gave J.J. a choice of last names. His choice would settle the issue. Keeping the name given to him in a Tulsa hospital years ago, he remained a Conley.

The Tulsa Public Schools system in the 1950s was under attack by two young students who, admittedly, were keen to have the attention of the class through look-at-me antics. According to Conley, future actor Gailard Sartain and he were in constant trouble. By their seventh grade, the administration had had enough. With a touch of mischievous humor, J.J. claimed that the two were "possibly responsible for numerous teacher resignations and we were idiots, [who] couldn't read, couldn't write. They told our parents they did not care what was done with us except to find a new school system and not put us in the same school."

As a result, Sartain enrolled at Cascia Hall, while Conley was admitted to the Oklahoma Military Academy. J.J. explains, "I was going to become an officer and he was going to be a Catholic."

"I've known Jerry for what seems like an eon," reports Sartain. He recalled J.J.'s "flair for the things that shouldn't be done in civilized society.

"Yes, I was a willing accomplice in some nefarious endeavors," he adds, "Wonderful memories."

Joining the army and eloping at seventeen with his eighteen-year-old girlfriend was a jolt to J.J.'s parents.

"She could have been arrested," Conley says. "I thought I was going to die in Vietnam. I thought at least she would get some money, but we barely lasted until boot camp. She fell in love with another guy and is still married to him." J.J. headed to Vietnam for a tour of duty. After enduring enough hysteria to last a lifetime, Conley left the service and utilized his GI bill.

He attended three universities for short periods of time. After racing a motorcycle up and down the fourth floor of Cordell dormitory in Stillwater, Conley claims that the OSU president personally advised him that he was no longer welcome in Stillwater. UCLA is barely a memory, but Conley stayed at Loyola for a semester before becoming disenchanted with too many rules.

"I will be missing Vespers again," he told his Catholic friends.

Conley decided to follow the footsteps of his grandpa and father, who were master journeymen. His grandpa was the master carpenter at the San Francisco Opera House until he died. His grandma formed the first wardrobe union in California. Gaining his union card in the mid-1960s, J.J. became a master lighting technician, working on numerous CBS TV shows like *The Smothers Brothers*, the *Jonathon Winters Comedy Hour* and many others. The union sent him to work the setup and lighting board for the Joffrey Ballet and the 1968 Academy Awards, as well as working the nightclub shows of numerous big-name entertainers like the Four Seasons and the presidential campaign of Hubert Humphrey.

Rubbing elbows with scores of Hollywood types led J.J. to Topanga Canyon's eight-acre Elysian Fields, a hippie nudist colony that lasted through 2001. According to Roman and Greek mythology, Elysian Fields was the final resting place of the souls of the heroic and virtuous. For Conley, it could

As a lighting engineer during his Hollywood heydays, Conley ran the lighting board for the 1968 Academy Awards. *J.J. Conley.*

be said that his association with the clothing-optional people of the Elysian Fields smacked him with high adventure, 1960s freedoms and high times. A little bit of heaven and a little bit more of hell.

Along with his high-rolling L.A. compatriots, J.J. headed for decadent escapades in Spain and France. This band of beautiful people draped with gold chains, expensive sunglasses and great tans took to the streets of Pamplona, home of the stampeding bulls. Plied with nasty Fume de Toro brandy and other ingestible contraband, J.J. found himself on a mission to extricate a travel mate from the boarded-up, no-way-out corridor that would soon contain the thundering herd of beasts. When he reached his compadre, J.J. tried to reason with him, saying, "Let's do this another day."

Too late. The cannon noise ricocheted down the cobbled streets loud as a thunderclap. The hoofed mob would soon be upon them. Crouched in a doorway, clutching the wood with a desperate embrace, they survived the cacophony of snorts and screams. Finally, they were the only two left on that section of the street. Laughing, breathing heavily, safe. But they were unaware of the format. No one had shown them the rulebook.

Once the bulls reach the ring, they are released to careen back up the street, only to be taunted with rolled-up newspapers and red-colored fabrics. The tired bulls, drunk with rage, and the tormentors drunk with spirits confronted each other once more. J.J. joined others in the forbidden challenge of climbing aboard a confused, marauding creature. Battered, bleeding and spotted with excrement, the bulls proved nonnegotiable. The good news was the badges of blood and stool that soiled his clothing entitled J.J. to a night of free drinks before leaving for France.

Elysium Institute's membership in the American Sunbathing Association gave them a free pass to over two hundred domestic au naturale resorts in Europe. While in France, they soaked up the sunshine at the largest facility in the country. By the second day they had already overstayed their welcome. They were bid adieu for introducing the clientele to the pleasures of psychedelics and mingling with too many of the mademoiselles.

Conley returned to California clothed and careered. In the days to come, he would find it difficult to leave the Hollywood lifestyle and the house overlooking Ventura Boulevard, and he grew tired of meeting a new somebody every day. Additionally, the letters from Tulsa kept urging him home. He grew weary of the arrogance of the show business stars.

"When the blue spot is turned off they are nothing," he says.

In 1973, he returned home. He rented an old house at Seventh and Peoria and brought a little "Bohemia back to Tulsa." The result was a shop called the Rubicon that sold California-style jewelry and beads, as well as head shop materials like rolling papers.

Recognizing a need for wider rolling papers (for tobacco and such), J.J. created Tulsa Tops papers. They were one and a half times wider than standard papers and could be used in a rolling machine or rolled by hand. After gaining a trademark in New York, the product became a national winner, beating EZ Wider and all the other big boys. He eventually sold the paper rights to a tobacco company.

Recalling a quote from comedian Lenny Bruce, an LA acquaintance who said, "There is nothing sadder than an old hipster," Conley determined that he was getting too old to be a hippie. In 1983, he sold all the Rubicon fixtures and converted the space to the Dragon's Tree restaurant, which, according to its matchbook cover, provided "spirits, pleasure and cuisine." This short-lived effort made way for a highly successful speakeasy.

Named Ricco's Blue Rose, this low-profile bar enjoyed immense success during Oklahoma's drink-by-the-wink era of illegal alcohol sales. A logo, replete with his tipped hat and a blue rose, of Edgar G. Robinson, acting

In the 1970s, J.J. designed and distributed, some say, the finest rolling papers made. *J.J. Conley.*

legend of the 1940s, adorned the Ricco business card. When a gangster dies, the tradition was to send a blue rose. This edgy symbol got the tongues wagging. Business went from good to great.

"If my reputation got bad, I enhanced it. The more wicked you are, the more they want to come," J.J. said after another pull on his vino. "Naïve people believe just about anything. I am not selling drugs. I am selling liquor illegally, but we are just having fun." Getting into Ricco's was part of the intrigue.

The parking lot was in the back. The front door was locked, and the back door was electronically switched with video camera surveillance. Entrance was granted by flashing your blue, hard plastic membership card to the camera before a security person would permit access. Lacking a card, a pretty woman was seldom turned away. Just inside the door, an attention-getting sign requested that you "unload your gun and take off your ski mask before entering." Another let you know that once you left, you couldn't come back in. You stayed in or you stayed out.

Inside were the beautiful people. Prominent lawyers, doctors, executives and "only the prettiest women" were allowed into the joint. Many were Vietnam vets. They were a pretty tight group. J.J. never felt a need to carry a gun, and there was never a fight.

Ricco's was not a large facility. The main floor had two small bar tops and comfortable furniture. The walls still contain photos and messages from the many movie stars with whom J.J. cavorted or admired: John Wayne, Dean

J.J. sandwiched between two of his favorite adult-only dancers, Bambee and Dale.
J.J. Conley.

Martin and the Lone Ranger, for example. This was the "medicinal era," so it would not have been surprising if someone had a gram of cocaine or some disco biscuits in his pocket. Yet drugs were not pedaled there.

The police were suspicious. There had to be something illegal going on there. A vice cop ambled into the bar one sunny afternoon. He asked J.J. if he minded a little inspection. Told he had the run of the house, the uniformed man searched every room and every inch of the basement before heading to the second floor with hopes of a damning violation. The highlight of the tour for J.J. was the cop assuming an aggressive stance before throwing open the second-floor bathroom door as if there would be criminals hiding inside. The news report said the police investigation was complete, and no drug activity was uncovered.

The story spread across the city's newspapers and television news. The police received some heat from the public that they must have been too shallow in their investigation. There must be something going on at Ricco's. J.J. just let the story build. People clamored to become part of the scene. The cost of membership cards permitting the purchase of alcoholic drinks continued to go up.

Initially, the VIP membership cards at Ricco's were a few dollars, then $5, then $20 and finally topping out in the hundreds. When asked what he learned about the success of the rapidly escalating membership fees, Conley responded, "One born every minute. Did not matter what I charged; they just kept on coming."

Then liquor became legal. J.J. quit the business immediately, saying, "Well, this is no fun now!" So he reinvented his business again, this time as a restaurant. Hoping to "cultivate some culture," he served flaming escargot, steaks and other high-end foods. It did not take long before he pared this down to today's gourmet burger. Now many Tulsa high-end restaurants have such an offering, but J.J. always makes sure his is the most expensive.

His burgers, mostly rib-eye with a little chuck to hold them together, were the first gourmet hamburgers in Tulsa. The starter has shrimp, several vegetable pieces in a delicious sticky seeded dressing and various nibble-sized crackers. The main course is, of course, the succulent burger, but wait, there is more: a cup of sweet baked beans, one perfectly smoked rib, thinly sliced cucumber and cantaloupe...and more. The final experience is a decadent chocolate brownie with walnuts and cappuccino. But take heed regarding the ordering process, or you will be rebuffed, although very politely.

Let's back up. On a small entry table rests a placard that tells you to be prepared to show your membership card. What? The card can be procured at the conclusion of your first dining experience. Not before. Maybe not at all.

This is J.J.'s domain. It is an autocracy. Remember that he is the Burger Nazi, and you will go far. If customers stroll in with bad hygiene, random piercings, loads of tattoos, tank tops or other offensive manner of dress, they will be asked for their membership card. Since they do not have one, they are reminded this is a member-only burger café. Mystified by the announcement, they stumble out into the street, hungry. On the way out, there is the sign that says, "Take this man to McDonalds. They have crayons there."

Further, it is important to understand his business plan. The café is open Tuesday through Friday, eleven to one only. There was a limit of fifty burger presentations each day, but that has been reduced to twenty-five. It was just too busy. Once sold, the kingdom closes for the day. Also, no credit cards or checks are accepted. In addition, don't ask to split an order with your spouse or request the burger to be cooked to your preferred doneness. No chance on either. Those and similar requests will get this smiling response, "You know, right up there at Fifteenth and Peoria are several places that will cook and serve your meal any way you want." The arrogant, standoffish attitude is a hook. It works.

In 1980, J.J. ended phone service to the café. Around 1990, there was a glowing article in the *Tulsa World* about J.J.'s Gourmet Burger Café. The response was incredible. Patrons were lined up out the door and down the sidewalk. Conley reacted by closing for a week, hoping they would all go away, and reduced his parking lot by half. Smiling, J.J. declares, "I have done everything I can to slow business down, and it has not worked.

"Occasionally some Gomer comes in here and wants me to burn up his burger. I just won't do it. Gomer tells me, 'That's bad fur yer bidness.' I tell him, 'Works for me.' The criticism is just the price you pay for glory."

The sole server is J.J. himself, and his longtime friend and employee Bernie Burt handles the cooking chores. J.J. takes your order or delivers his pronouncements of no-can-do dressed very smartly. Conley is a clotheshorse. He recalls the day when people would wear a tie to go to the Will Rogers Theatre to watch a film. Presumably, both he and Sartain took off their fancy duds before digging tunnels in Conley's backyard as they reenacted every action movie shown at the theatre situated just across the street.

Las Vegas dealers used to wear tuxedos. Now they wear parachute pants and flip-flops. J.J. won't go.

"I can dress casually," he says, "but if I go out or go to somebody else's place, I don't want to embarrass them."

He started out with the button-down, Ivy League style and just stuck with it, saying, "I am never going to wear a JC Penney blazer and wingtips again. So I overdo it. So what? It is my only Jones. I don't bowl, have kids or chase women. All I have is me, so if me wants to dress nice, it is quite a bit less expensive than other habits."

He used to play golf, but now there are just a bunch of poorly dressed guys playing instead of smartly dressed business types. So he nailed his

J.J., on the right, with the author at Conley's no-nonsense gourmet burger café. *Author collection.*

Ping clubs to the restaurant wall. People comment on how nice they are. Conley tells them, "I want to cut them up and throw them away." It just drives them crazy.

For years, J.J. has ordered all his clothes online. He likes the English style, including the watch fob and other gold chains. Conley is a huge fan of Italian suits with angled hacking suit pockets and split vents.

"Anyway," he laments, "they don't make my size [for regular retail]. I'm a dwarf!" But he looks good.

He looks good all the way to the bank as well. Conley says he'll never change the business again. It's too good, and everybody likes it.

"I'll just stay with it," he says.

Chapter 11

HARRY F. SINCLAIR

The Trouble with Harry

S enator Thomas J. Walsh of Montana bent over the library table, peered down at witness Harry Ford Sinclair, and said, "I wish you would tell us about a contract you made touching the Teapot Dome scandal."

Sinclair whispered into the ear of his attorney, regarded his reply and turned toward his inquisitor. A bulky, some would say strongly built, man—with his slightly oversized head topped with the fedoras of the day, and his frame girded with the expensive suits suited to a man of his stature—he merely scoffed. Then, with the swagger of a Clan Macgregor tossing an enemy's head onto a battle pitch, Sinclair squared up and said, "Senator, I decline to answer your impertinent question."

Impertinent, maybe, but the senator held the cards. It was March 1924, and Sinclair was sitting before the Senate Committee on Public Lands. Committee members asked ten questions regarding his suspect behavior uncovered during his acquittal in an earlier fraud trial involving a felonious secretary of the interior. Harry remained smug, knowing that back home, all those oil pumpers in the Mid-Continent field were making him millions. Sinclair was equally at home doing vodka shots with Russian czars and strolling oil derrick grime. But he did not coddle or cotton. He expected orders to be executed and respected friendship only if deserved.

His respect for the United States Senate was contentious. A year earlier, a *New York Times* front-page headline in January 1923 declared, "Sinclair Refuses Records to Senate; Oil Man Defies the La Follette Committee to Delve into His Private Affairs; Fine and Prison Possible."

A smug and dapper Harry Sinclair poses on the steps of the United States Supreme Court. *Gerkin collection/Winnar Co.*

"Will you produce the records and books called for?" demanded Senator Robert La Follette of Wisconsin. "I will discuss the matter with my counsel and let you know later on," replied Sinclair, who was smiling despite the tenseness of the situation. He told the legislators, "I will go to the Supreme Court, if necessary," before submitting information about transactions he held personal and beyond the committee's interest. Sinclair walked out of the committee room, suddenly ending the investigative session.

After two hours, Sinclair remained sequestered in a private room of the senate wing with his attorneys—chief counsel J.W. Zevely of Washington, G.T. Stanford of New York and Judge A.N. Chandler of Tulsa. With time approaching the five o'clock bell, committee chairman La Follette issued a subpoena via the sergeant-at-arms. Sinclair and his legal team returned to the chambers shortly after the committee adjourned. La Follette "refused to say whether Mr. Sinclair would be judged in contempt and thus made liable to fine or imprisonment or both."

Sinclair was willing to roll the dice.

Harry Sinclair gambled the family drugstore to finance an oil lease and lost. Penniless, he shot his toe hunting rabbits, had it amputated and collected

$5,000 from an insurance claim. Some say he did it on purpose, while Harry said it made for a good yarn.

Sinclair used his coverage proceeds to buy lumber, selling it to the wildcatters who constructed pyramid-shaped structures on the oil patches springing up in the Mid-Continent fields of southeast Kansas. He learned that, with little risk, he could turn a small investment into a big dividend. With that, twenty-one-year-old Harry Ford Sinclair was in the oil business.

By his mid-twenties, Sinclair supervised forty wildcats from his three-room office above the Independence, Kansas post office. Forming single-lease companies for his many sponsors, Sinclair was the manager and usually the treasurer, often earning seventy-five dollars a month, and he always insisted on absolute control. After grabbing a few shares for his diligent work, the promoters sold quickly when the wells began to yield oil. Sinclair was the bird dog for rich speculators. His rate of success was uncanny. Pleasing his shareholders with his knack for site selection, Sinclair turned fast, if sometimes small, profits while developing a managerial style of quick decisions, absolute control, infectious zeal and voluminous pluck. Said one of his East Coast backers: "He calls us together occasionally to tell us what he's done. He is shrewd but hearty, tough but genial, a masterful trader, a hard-driving sportsman."

Sinclair attracted the attention of wealthy speculators like Chicago meatpacker J.M. Cudahy, Pittsburgh capitalist Theodore Barnsdall and James F. O'Neill, president of Prairie Oil Company, a subsidiary of John D. Rockefeller's Standard Oil of Kansas. Unlike his backers, Sinclair came from humble beginnings.

Harry Ford Sinclair was born in 1876 near Wheeling, West Virginia. The federal census of 1880 lists his father, John Sinclair, as a druggist and his mother, Phoebe, a housewife. The family headed west when Harry was young, settling in Independence, Kansas. John opened a drugstore, intending that his son become part of the family business. To that end, Sinclair graduated from the University of Kansas with a pharmacology degree. But oil proved to be a more seductive drug.

Banks more familiar with farmers, ranchers and merchants were reluctant to fund black-gold prospecting. Sinclair realized that, at least in the short run, he needed to finance his own deals. After a decade prowling for undervalued oil leases across Kansas and the Indian Territory, Harry hit it big with a strike in the rich Kiowa field that made him a millionaire before his thirtieth birthday.

When oil blew in 1905 at the farm of Ida Glenn south of Tulsa, Sinclair raced there from Independence and snatched up premium leases before prices rocketed. News spread of the bountiful Glenn Pool (it ultimately yielded 340 million barrels of crude), and the place grew thick with wells and "corner shooters," who leased up property adjacent to a producing lease, usually on the corners, in order to leech from the known pool or formation.

The magnitude of oil that arrived at the surface presented huge storage issues. "Get it fast and get it first" was the mantra—and figure out what to do with it later. Lease operators like the Sinclairs pumped crude into hastily constructed storage tanks and large, earthen, environment-be-damned lakes. Oil fouled streams and underground aquifers. Tank farms frequently burned, creating Red Adair–style fire hazards. Corner shooters and the "rule of capture" reigned—seven years later, the Glenn pool was dry. But not before Harry Sinclair made millions.

The territory gushers ushered in an era of big banking. Lew Wentz, the Phillips brothers, Harry Sinclair and a host of other wealthy oilmen believed banks to be sound investments. The effect of the oil industry working in concert with financial institutions was to create staggering economic growth. Yet there were periods of banking turmoil.

The young, restless Oklahoma economy rose and fell with the volatile price of crude. Lax regulations permitted banks the risky business of acquiring smaller banks. If economic conditions or poor management caused a subsidiary bank to suffer from depositor panic, mass withdrawals were a deathblow, resulting in a negative ripple affect on the consumer confidence of the owner bank. Wildcatter E.F. Blaise formed the oil-industry-friendly Farmer's National Bank of Tulsa in 1903. Subsequently, Farmer's bought the Kiefer State Bank that sprung up close to the Glenn Pool.

The Kiefer bank failed in February 1910. Feeling the onslaught of withdrawals from the Exchange stimulated by the Kiefer collapse, Blaise and his wildcatting business partner, Tulsa attorney C.J. Wrightsman, called an emergency nighttime meeting of selected Tulsa oilmen for later that day.

No sooner had the men exited the room did Sinclair, P.J. White, James Chapman and Robert McFarlin buy Farmer's, changing its name to Exchange National Bank and installing Sinclair as the new president. Harry Sinclair was now a bank owner.

The chief counsel for the Exchange National bank was Joseph L. Hull Sr., the grandfather of Tulsa entrepreneur and attorney Joe Hull III. His office on Cheyenne Avenue sits across the street from the site of Sinclair's Tulsa residence. "The interesting thing about Grandpa," Hull said, leaning back into his leather chair, looking out his office window, "was that he was blind, blinded by an optic nerve disease that today would easily be treated with antibiotics. He had a reader and learned Braille." His grit was a perfect match for Sinclair. The bank, juggling needs with risks, was poised for the next uptick in oil activity.

As Farmer's National, it was the most influential bank in Oklahoma; under new management, Exchange survived from an unprecedented policy of personally guaranteeing each dollar deposited. But the challenges of the Great Depression brought hard times. Thankfully, the onus of guaranteed deposits ended with the passage of the far-reaching Glass-Steagall Act of 1933, which, among other things, protected depositors and restricted the speculation arm of banks from owning other financial institutions. (The act was ultimately repealed in 1999.)

Undeterred, Sinclair, Chapman and others reorganized the Exchange National Bank as the National Bank of Tulsa in 1933, establishing its global reputation as the "Oil Bank of America." Enlarging the 1917 construction of the ten-story Exchange building, the elaborate National Bank edifice included a dirigible mooring at the top of its middle section. Years later, the landmark building at 320 South Boston became the Bank of Oklahoma. One block east of the Exchange was a luxurious counterpart.

Any deal worth doing was done in the Hotel Tulsa, built in 1912 at Third and Cincinnati. The fifth floor was Sinclair's lair. He commuted daily via train from Independence for all-night poker games, whiskey drinking and deal making—including the formation of the Sinclair-White Oil Company. But the Exchange Bank and the Oklahoma oil fields proved too small for the big nature of Sinclair. He headed for New York. Firmly planted, his new address granted him immediate access to the power brokers.

In the fall of 1916, after meeting with Wall Street investors and attorneys, Sinclair announced a $50 million deal: the consolidation of five hundred miles of pipelines, big-capacity refineries, the Cudahy marketing facilities and personal control of 532 wells with the potential to produce 5.5 million barrels of oil a year. Sinclair borrowed another $20 million to procure undervalued assets in the Mid-Continent Oil Province. Sinclair Oil and Refining Company secured a charter "in perpetuity" from New York State on May 1, 1916.

Sinclair maintained his presence in Tulsa by building the eight-story Sinclair Building at Fifth and Main Streets, circa 1919, plus the brick home at 1730 South Cheyenne for his wife, Elizabeth, and two children, in the shade of the Creek Council Oak tree.

Located just outside the surveyed city limits of Tulsa on what was formerly Lochpoka's ceremonial square, Sinclair, his brother Earl—who handled

Harry built the grand, eight-story Sinclair Building in downtown Tulsa in 1919. *Beryl Ford Collection/Rotary Club and Tulsa Historical Society.*

many of Sinclair's business finances—Josh Cosden and others made quick order of greatly undervalued lots of a former Creek allotment purchased by important Tulsa real estate developer Grant Stebbins from the heir of Wehiley Neharkey.

Years later, his multistory mansion would fall to make way for an upscale condominium complex, but in its day, Sinclair was big—big enough to threaten Rockefeller. Traveling by private aircraft, he thumbed his nose at earthbound competitors. A few months shy of forty, the magnate was near the top of the Big Oil elite. One of them, Edward Doheny, became his intimate friend.

He shared with Sinclair the mechanics of doing business in New York and Washington, D.C. In 1921, Doheny confidentially bragged that he had his son deliver $100,000 in a little black bag to Interior Secretary of State Albert Hall, greasing the awarding of a no-bid lease of the fertile Elk Hill, a wealth of California oil reserves owned by the federal government.

The success of Doheny's business tactic encouraged Sinclair, who learned about a no-bid lease opportunity for the federal Teapot Dome in Wyoming, a federal reserve set aside for use by the United States naval fleet. The reserve was named after a desolate, windblown expanse in Wyoming whose landscape featured a rock vaguely resembling a teapot. Sinclair sent a deliveryman to Secretary Fall's office armed with $200,000 in a handbag, along with his best regards to the 1920 presidential campaign of Warren G. Harding. The lease went to Sinclair, and his company spent $35 million dollars on the operation.

Sinclair took his show on the road. In the early 1920s, he led an entourage of eighty to Russia for a personal meeting with Lenin to discuss obtaining oil rights in Siberia, promising to raise money by bond issues. Meanwhile, trouble was brewing in Gotham.

Interior Secretary Fall had been indicted for fraud as a result of his black-bag transactions with Doheny and Sinclair, who were subsequently and similarly charged. Fall was convicted—the first felony for a public federal official while in office. After a lengthy trial, Doheny was acquitted of bribing the secretary. During the three years between being charged with fraud and his trial, Sinclair continued directing his empire.

His first trial was declared a mistrial when it was exposed that Sinclair had hired detectives to follow jurymen. A second resulted in his acquittal, but a U.S. Senate committee would not let go of the jury-shadowing incident. The entire ordeal dragged out for seven years. Not one to hide behind the Fifth—the due process amendment to the Constitution regarding self-incrimination—Sinclair testified before *twelve* separate legislative committees. On advice of counsel, he failed to answer one question. Sinclair and his attorney reasoned it irrelevant regarding another man's testimony concerning the Teapot Dome investigation, which was already in the Congressional records—and it cost him.

That omission landed Sinclair in the Washington, D.C. House of Detention, guilty of contempt of the senate. With subsequent appeals to the Supreme Court unsuccessful, Sinclair served six and a half months in 1929.

Robert L. Owen, a Muskogee native, served Oklahoma as a United States senator during the time of the Teapot Dome lease and investigation. Responding to a written request by Harry Rogers of the Exchange National Bank, asking for his views on the merit of the suits brought against Sinclair, Owen wrote a lengthy review in the as-lengthily titled *Remarkable Experiences of H.F. Sinclair with His Government: Some Dangerous Precedents.*

Owen wrote, "As a witness, Sinclair had been denied the right to have the constitutionality or pertinence of a question determined before punishment can be imposed upon him for refusal to answer. He was given six months in jail for criminal contempt of court, for an act in which he violated no law of Congress, no law of the United States, no existing rule of court, for an act, which had been practiced by the government and private individuals for 30 years."

The Senate committee decided that the hiring of a detective agency by Sinclair to shadow his trial jurors at a distance, without them being aware of their presence, obstructed the administration of justice. "The court thus holds that it was a contempt of its authority for people outside the court house to keep an unknown watch on jurymen (to ensure no one approached and influenced them), and that such observation obstructed the administration of justice," wrote Owen. The court in violation of reason did hold this contemptible. "This flat declaration that what did not obstruct justice did obstruct justice is equivalent to saying, that white is black," he concluded.

Sinclair got out in November 1929, just in time for the advent of the Great Depression and a tempest in Oklahoma. "I was railroaded to jail in violation of common sense and common fairness," he shouted, storming out of the detention facility, continuing, "I cannot be contrite for sins for which I know I have never committed."

An early post-detention business move involved Sinclair selling his pipeline subsidiary to his rival, Standard Oil Company, to have ready cash for buying flagging companies. The Sinclair group grew substantially during 1930–36, acquiring companies and properties for pennies on the dollar. Oil prospecting "was not an industry but a gamble," said Tom Slick and oilmen did not cotton to government playing a hand.

"Oklahoma oilmen avoided control by the government which was seen as unwarranted interference with their liberties," said Bruce Niemi, author of *The Greatest Individual Act,* "with Sinclair squaring off against Governor

Sinclair gas stations still dot the Tulsa landscape. The signature logo, Dino the dinosaur, remains the marketing graphic atop store signs. *Gerkin collection.*

'Alfalfa Bill' Murray in 1930–1931. The oil industry overproduced the Mid-Continent Oil Province during the 1920s in an atmosphere of inter-industry cooperation or 'associationalism,' thus depressing petroleum prices."

As the issues became worse, the governor took dead aim at Sinclair and his fellow producers, threatening to shut down most Oklahoma wells so that production would cease for a period of time, allowing for prices to improve and creating more tax money for the state's education program. Challenged by the threat of an oilmen injunction, Murray erupted, "It'll be like a jackrabbit trying to tree a wild cat."

Sinclair responded by opening the pipeline valves, saying, "Wide open production would soon kill off some of the weaklings, leaving the strong to get together with some chance of staying together."

The governor responded in kind by declaring martial law on August 4, 1931 (it lasted sixty-five days). "Murray installed a distant cousin, Cicero Murray, to be the 'Generalissimo' of the troops deployed to the oil fields," stated Niemi. The Generalissimo's Major Herskowitz stood atop the crown block of an oil well, shouting out the orders, "Lieutenant, take a squad and shut in those Sinclair wells." By year end, oil prices rose to the desired price of two dollars a barrel, and martial law was lifted. "Alfalfa Bill" declared his decision to be "the greatest individual act of my life."

Niemi claims, "'Alfalfa Bill' drove Sinclair out of Oklahoma," chasing him to his mansion on Long Island. Undaunted, his uncompromising spirit continued to drive his company in new directions with continued success. He was a walking poster child of American business swagger.

Sinclair netted $81 million in 1948, producing nearly forty million barrels of crude. It was time to rest. He retired in 1949 at the age of seventy-three. He walked away from an enterprise worth $700 million, nearly 100,000 stockholders and twenty-one thousand employees. His ferocious ambition, audacity and individualism left a deeply embedded legacy.

Sinclair died in Pasadena, California, seven years later. Many were surprised at the death notice of the legend. They thought he was already gone.

Chapter 12

HAY IS FOR HOSSES

*A Hay Hauler Fights Drought and Technology
to Preserve a Pastime*

K elly Cox towered over the loader with its arriving bale, wielding a hay hook in each hand like a pirate of the plains, ready to stab the end of each parcel of dried grasses and sling it into place on the flatbed of his hay truck. He shouted over the mechanical din, "Life can't get any better than this." But in fact, it should.

It's another August harvest south of Bixby, and Cox grins in spite of the grim reality that debilitating drought had stunted the prime time for grass growing, nearly eliminating the largest of the usual three-crop season. A recent half-inch of rain nourished the parched shoots, creating a small growth spurt, enough to warrant cutting and baling. Cox, his helper Kurtis and wife, Joyce, made hay.

Joyce drove his '56 Ford slowly down the row of baled hay, lining up the loader that snatched each bale and raised it up to the deck of the flatbed. The crunch of the big, black tires as they rolled over the stubble of the shorn grasses created a sound like crumpling paper. The dryness of the earth produced a haze of fine dust that partially shrouded the truck and crew.

The hay making its way up the loader was Haygrazer (a Sudan and sorghum hybrid) grass planted after the last freeze with a grain drill pulled behind the tractor, relying on gravity to feed the seed into the ground. Alfalfa is planted in the fall and harvested in May and then, depending on rainfall, is cropped up to five times. On average, alfalfa provides three cutting opportunities. Yet the dryness of 2012 yielded only two cuttings of any kind of hay.

The Cox hay truck trundles down his mowed hayfield while lifetime friend Curtis takes a breather. *Gerkin collection.*

Quick to laugh and prone to jawboning, punctuating everything with gestures, Cox kept a near-constant monologue with his longtime buddy Kurtis. They were moving hay bales like the farmers of the old days, sweating and content.

Cox was attracted to hay hauling for the girls—the bronze tans and Popeye arms of the boy haulers who got all the ladies. He mounted his first hay truck at age twelve, working with his brother and taking orders from his dad. Scared to death, he shouldered the wheel, applying farmer's work ethics learned in his early years with a surrogate family.

In the late 1950s, there were no day-care centers in rural Oklahoma. Cox's mom worked as a secretary for various oil companies, while his dad, Joseph

Eschewing modern, rolled-bale technology, Kelly Cox stands on the bed of his hay truck, poised to snatch a square hay bale. *Gerkin collection.*

Franklin Cox Jr., farmed hay. An unruly two-year-old Cox shuffled between a host of babysitters incapable of corralling his spirit. Then he bunked at the house of his father's friend, Otis Hullsenbeck, who kept the young boy until he was seven years old.

On Leonard Mountain, there were only woods, cows, pastures and hillbillies like Otis. The coon dog trainer and his charge spent most of their days outside, riding horses and becoming big pals. Cox, innocent to the primitive living conditions (he took his baths in a No. 7 metal washtub), learned the backwoods life. He helped Otis and his wife pull water from a well with a rope and bucket, dug up potatoes they stored in the earth outside the front door and helped raise coon dogs for sale. "He told me about Jesse James hiding treasures in nearby caves and treated me like a son," Cox recalled.

Back on the family farm, the youth became a trusted hand. Under a photo of Cox from that era, his mom inscribed, "Kelly was different—always wants to be outside." Their living conditions were relatively Spartan; the temperature inside the house was the same as outside. "We didn't have a thermostat until I was seventeen," Cox said. "If I left a glass of water on the counter on a winter night, it was frozen by morning. Didn't think anything of it."

Cox lived with his grandparents during the week while going to school in Bixby. The creature comforts there were likewise sparse. When his Grandpa made it clear that baths were only permitted on Saturdays, Cox said, "I yelled, 'Whoo-hooooo.'" Near the end of one week, he started losing hearing in one ear. The physician cleaned the dirt pile from his ear and made a diagnosis: he had a bean growing in it. Cox recalled a reporter from the Bixby paper taking a picture of him.

Grandpa Cox was his buddy. They'd rock on a front porch swing, the ten-year-old listening as his mentor extolled the virtues of telling the truth, helping friends and strangers and other life lessons, the same ones ingrained in his father.

His father developed incurable lung cancer from a lifetime of cigarette smoking. Now a Bixby sophomore, Cox dropped baseball so he could take up the slack. He paid the pecan pickers, tended the pigs and maintained the equipment. His brother and sister pitched in where they could. When his dad passed, his daily slopping of the pigs that he enjoyed because "I get a kick out of watching pigs eat" became secondary to managing the family business, which included the hay crop.

With his mother's help, seventeen-year-old Cox borrowed money to buy a 1959 Chevy Viking truck and a hay bale loader. He and his buddies joked that the Bixby girls took notice. "I started the business for all the wrong reasons," said Cox, laughing, "but we're still doing it today."

He's the last left working the old homestead farm his ancestors tilled before him. His parents harvested pecan trees that still wind their way through the property, sacking the nuts in a small barn north of the house. They grew tomatoes, cantaloupes and watermelons. The pigs rutted until the big trucks came and took them away. The Cox brood counted on all the fruits of the land, but hay ruled the roost.

Except for his years at Oklahoma State University, Cox has lived on and worked the same piece of dirt. He came home each summer to manage the hay crop. He always had to hire a hay helper for the summer. On a bulletin board at the OSU agriculture department, Cox posted a summer job opportunity: "Get a tan, build your muscles, see the country, get away from the rat race." A personable martial arts aficionado named Clay Williams took the bait. The business needs soon required more than a summer helper.

In the late 1970s, at the height of his hay-hauling days, Cox had four trucks and up to fifteen employees. He paid them three to five cents a bale, and typically they processed eight hundred bales a day, but sometimes it was as many as two thousand. The hay truck was the critical employee.

He recently sold the original Chevy. Now, his go-to truck is a 1956 Ford F-600 once owned by a farmer named Earl Clayton. Cox lusted for that truck for more than a decade, but Earl would not let it go. It was parked behind Earl's barn, full of manure and with a cracked windshield. When Earl retired, he sold it to a horse rancher.

Cox tracked the owner down fifteen years ago and bought the hay truck for $750 cash and $450 worth of hay. Hauling the Ford down the six-lane highway to Leonard—knowing it had only thirty-three thousand miles on it but mindful that it badly needed paint, tires, brakes and insurance—he mused that the number of hayfields may have diminished, but the old hay truck had survived. Still, it has been assaulted.

Once, after a hot day of hauling hay, the door handle jammed. Cox moved to the passenger side and tried to kick the door open. He dented the metal door panel entrapping the lowered window. The door did not open. Unconsciously, he reached for the handle, gave it a gentle lift, and the door swung open. Years later, he uses a vice-grip to crank open the window. The rusted grip hangs forlornly. The wipers still do not wipe. "Who needs them?" he said. "If it is raining, we're not hauling hay anyway."

Over the years, agricultural technology improved the business economy of hauling hay, reducing the number of workers needed to harvest

Kelly Cox steps into his cherished '56 Ford. Vice grips serve as the window crank. *Gerkin collection.*

and bale the dry grasses. By 1992, the advent of the round baler machine towed behind a tractor made it possible for a single worker to cut and bale the hay into huge round bales, leaving them in the field with no need for barn storage and the requisite hay hauler. Traditional hay harvesting creates square, relatively porous bales, which are stored in barns—necessary to prevent up to 50 percent decomposition from rain. Round bales can be left in the field due to their baling process. "Rain penetrates (a round bale) only a small way into the hay, so the loss is considerably less," Cox explained.

The price tag of $35,000 for the round baler requires at least one thousand acres of hay, Cox said. The round baler put an end to the days of custom hauling for ranches and large farms. Today, the old homestead is Cox's only source of hay. No longer needing a fleet of trucks and hands, he's back to his original staffing of one truck and one helper.

Over the years, Cox has gone through four chiropractors and five massage therapists. "Only by the grace of God," he said, "am I still doing it." He was born again in 1986 after reading a windshield pamphlet. He took the literature to his room in the farmhouse he shared with his mother, poring over the sinner's prayer. Cox confessed, "God was speaking right to me." A baptism followed, and he changed his carousing and drinking ways.

With fewer and fewer people needing him to haul their hay, Cox repairs oil well pump jacks part time. Joyce is a computer systems analyst for American Electric Power. They raise okra, watermelons, new potatoes and tomatoes, selling them during the summer at the Broken Arrow farmer's market for extra revenue.

Cox staves off "driving into an asphalt jungle and sitting in a chair all day for my occupation," remaining romantic about turning grasses into square bales. "Why should I stay with it?" he said with a laugh. "I doubt it's for the money!"

Chapter 13

PLANET OF THE MUSHROOMS

A Fungi Odyssey

When the tree leaves turn, some folks think of foliage tours. But Oklahoma foodies and chefs look earthward for the real fall treats: mushrooms. Although examples of these edible fungi are available most of the year, we tend to think of them as a fall sport. There are those gastronomes who don't need deciduous forests or seasonal changes to enjoy this meaty, flavorful treat. They just need resources that provide nature's hidden treasure.

Preferring forests and frequent rains, mushrooms like chanterelles and the treasured morels thrive in the green hills of eastern Oklahoma. Surprisingly, other varieties are flourishing where the sun don't shine. Shittake, oysters and other mushroom varieties find indoor settings favorable for cultivation. Indoor mushroom farming is a burgeoning adventure, and there are groups of organic-minded farmers scattered all over the state.

One such couple is Tulsans Sharon and Rich Hewitt. Together they own Mushroom Planet. Certified organic by the Oklahoma Department of Agriculture, these indoor farmers have amazed shroomers for over a decade, providing a variety of world-class mushrooms that grow in the friendly confines of their seventy-square-foot, environmentally controlled basement farm. You can grow them on wood chips, straw and even on toilet paper called Tee Pee Farms. The Hewitt "shroomery," located just north of downtown Tulsa, is free of the usual farm pests, birds and unpredictable weather patterns. No tractors, no fertilizers and no traditional soil are part of the couple's endeavor.

Pioneer indoor mushroom farmer Rich Hewitt holds a growth of mushrooms cultivated in his specially designed basement. *Photo courtesy of This Land Press.*

Instead, there's sawdust. As a basis for indoor agriculture, mushroom farmers reclaim this waste product by using it as their soil. The Hewitts seed a hard oak sawdust block with mushroom mycelium, turning each block into its own farm. Their basement facility features a carefully controlled temperature and humidity environment. Amateur growers place a plastic bag over wooden pegs that are used as miniature tent poles, creating a microclimate for each farm. Growth-producing incandescent lights shine on the farms, creating an eerie panorama of glowing domes evocative of an extraterrestrial landscape.

After harvest, the sawdust blocks and their organic grains are recycled as compost for future crops. The Hewitts' sawdust garden sprouts shiitakes, maitakes, lion's mane, oyster and golden oyster mushrooms for their adoring fans. Statewide, local farmers like Rich and Sharon have banded together.

The Oklahoma Food Cooperative is a vital link to those who passionately care about their agricultural goods and an appreciative community that supports them. It only sells food and non-food products that are made in Oklahoma via an order delivery system based on its website, along with a network of members and volunteers across the state. Each month, producer members post on the cooperative's website what they have available.

No matter how you source your mushrooms, ultimately, it may be their final destination that matters most. As pluperfect ingredients for thousands of recipes and restaurant menus, food freaks and chefs fantasize about their earthy goodness. Imagine improving your immune system through the ingesting of this edible fungus. Imagine this irresistible source of flavor, texture and aroma in tortellini in a chanterelle broth, miso shitake breakfast soup or a shellfish risotto with mushrooms. Just imagine.

Foodies and professionals savor dreams of a great pinot noir with its earthy flavor notes, especially when it is paired with coddled eggs and porcini or any mushroom offering. It is ethereal to many. It reminds the oenophile that the wine in the glass is a force of nature, much like the enduring mushroom itself. Often, pinot noir is considered the ultimate wine: silky, sexy and seductive. Just like the storied 'shroom.

Chapter 14

THE RINGLEADER

The Burning of the Coliseum and the End of Tulsa Wrestling's Romantic Era

In a promotional piece, the Tulsa Underground Circus actors fictitiously wrote that it was the work of a deranged Russian immigrant, a circus clown trained at the Moscow Circus School. They created the saga that the day before the real-life, catastrophic Tulsa Coliseum fire, during a routine inspection of the show's equipment, the fire marshal found disturbing evidence that he felt required legal interrogation. Within several of the trunks were sheaths of human skin and a cadaver with a paper maché face. The marshal cancelled the group's impending Coliseum debut, locking up all circus possessions inside the building and throwing the Ruskie into a rage. The marketing blurb continued that he perished in the fire, or perhaps he returned to Siberia. Either way, he disappeared. The truth is that smoke and mirrors were no strangers to Tulsa's Coliseum.

In the golden age of "Killers" and "Stranglers," "Gorgeous George" Wagner, holding a PhD in psychology, was professional wrestling's pretty boy. Wagner had a valet who would disinfect the ring—spraying it with perfume and sprinkling rose petals across its mat—before curly, blond Gorgeous would make his entrance, stepping through the ropes like some Liberace of the turnbuckles. He was a taunted coward whose shtick made him rich and famous in a Tulsa landmark known as the Avey Coliseum. In the 1940s, wrestling in Tulsa was a wildly popular attraction, with crowds cramming and jamming the art deco Coliseum—it sat a few blocks from the BOK, where today the WWE holds similar court—and Wagner was part of a stable.

Cavernous and decadent, the memory of the building is shared by few. Tulsa developer and politico Sharon King-Davis, a granddaughter of Avey,

The largest show palace in the southwest, the Coliseum was in the heart of downtown Tulsa. *Beryl Ford Collection/Rotary Club and Tulsa Historical Society.*

recalls going to a midget wrestling card as a young girl with her mom, Pat, who shared a fifty-fifty ownership of the building with her dad, Sam Avey. Sitting on the front row when the smaller-size gladiators wildly pulled themselves through the ropes and onto the mat, the crowd erupted, and she remembers, "I was so scared, I ran up the aisle and wouldn't come back."

Avey, a native of Kingfisher, traveled six years in the 1910s with vaudeville companies, learning how to put on a show. With the popularity of professional wrestling on the rise, the sport seemed like a sure bet. Shortly after World War I, Avey went on tour as a referee for the successful promoter Billy Sandow.

Armed with his insider knowledge, Avey moved his family to Tulsa in 1924 to launch a new venture for Sandow. With the prowess of the Oklahoma A&M wrestling program, the state had become a mecca for aspiring wrestlers. But there was nowhere to stage matches.

In the mid-1920s, a Minnesota native named Walter Whiteside founded the Douglas Oil Company with money he made as a lumber mogul in

Washington state and British Columbia. But Whiteside had dreams beyond liquid gold. With F.S. Stryker, he formed the Magic City Amusement Co. and, in 1928, built an indoor arena on the west side of Elgin Avenue extending the entire block from Sixth to Fifth Streets.

Designed by architect Leon Senter—whose projects include Skelly Stadium, Booker T. Washington High School and St. John Hospital—the 7,500-seat brick and terra-cotta edifice was the largest show palace of the Southwest. Its floor could be iced over in eight hours, making it the region's first indoor skating rink, the primary interest of Whiteside.

The Coliseum opened on New Year's Day 1929, with the Tulsa Oilers playing their first American Hockey Association game against the Duluth Hornets, thus accomplishing Whiteside's goal of establishing the city as the southernmost frontier of professional hockey. Interestingly, the Hornets were the first athletic club sponsored by Whiteside and his father in their hometown of Duluth. Sam Avey, watching from a different set of sidelines, had his eye on the new venue for a different sort of sport.

Sam Avey, front left, with Coliseum wrestlers, owned the Coliseum for its last decade. *Beryl Ford Collection/Rotary Club and Tulsa Historical Society.*

The Depression came and wiped out Whiteside's thriving empire. His holdings, including the Coliseum, went into receivership for a decade. Then, in 1942, creditors formed the Coliseum Company and bought the property in a sheriff's auction. Tulsans—war-torn and downtrodden—took heart.

Avey claimed he had to pawn his favorite shirt and go deeper in debt than he liked when he purchased the Coliseum for $185,000 in 1944. The electric organ continued to pump out the "Skater's Waltz" as thousands learned to ice-skate, and locals packed the house to hear Nat King Cole. But nothing drew crowds like the shirtless men in tights.

Doing what he did best, Avey popularized Monday night wrestling long before Howard Cosell, Frank Gifford and "Dandy" Don Meredith proved America was ready for some football. With its outlandish personalities and questionable ethics, wrestling was all the rage. Avey promoted his favorite arena-filling star, Leroy McGuirk.

The former Oklahoma A&M standout became the U.S. junior heavyweight wrestling champ. Professional wrestlers flocked to the Avey Coliseum for a chance to take down McGuirk. The pro circuit hit the road, largely in the South. During a trip to Little Rock, McGuirk was blinded in a car wreck. Rather than

Center ring during a Coliseum wrestling match. *Beryl Ford Collection/Rotary Club and Tulsa Historical Society.*

abandon his franchise, Avey put McGuirk in the post of matchmaker and gave him a stake in his Tulsa-based promotion company.

The Coliseum welcomed the likes of Killer Kowalski, Ed "Strangler" Lewis—a beast of a man with big, black bushy eyebrows, monstrous hands and a thick neck out of proportion to his super-sized head—and a local yokel named Farmer Jones. Weighing in at over three hundred pounds, this Arkansas native in single-strapped overalls said to Frank Morrow of KRMG radio, "Once I git on top of 'em, they ain't goin' far." Yet the pleasinest' crowd pleaser of them all was Al "Spider" Galento.

The "Spider" would wrestle all comers—$1 for each minute you could stay in the ring with him and $100 if you won. Occasionally, Galento would become frustrated with his opponent and pummel him in the face, an illegal action that drew hisses and dismissals. Celebrating the unexpected victory, the bleacher bum staggered off the mat, waving

A major wrestling personality at the Colliseum was Spider Galento, 1952. *Beryl Ford Collection/Rotary Club and Tulsa Historical Society.*

the C-note. The cheers and jeers that followed him out would not echo for long.

At 9:31 p.m. on September 20, 1952—a Saturday—a three-alarm fire sent eleven fire trucks to a blaze engulfing the Coliseum.

Ray Murphy, living in an apartment directly across the street from the Coliseum, told television and newspaper reporters that just moments before noticing the fire on top of the building, he saw a lightning bolt flash above the structure. It had not rained for twenty-five days, and the wooden roof was dry as kindling.

The night watchman was due to report at 10:00 p.m., which meant only two people were in the building as it went up in flames.

KAKC, an Avey-owned station, had set up its studios in the building's basement. In its soundproof catacombs, DJ Bob Griffin, a University of Tulsa freshman, and chief engineer M.M. Donley were monitoring a broadcast of the Mutual Radio Network, having switched from the rain-cancelled stock car races at the Tulsa Fairgrounds. Water from the fire hoses gushed through the soaked ceiling. Griffin climbed the stairs to the street.

A 1952 lightning strike ignited the Coliseum's wooden roof. *Beryl Ford Collection/Rotary Club and Tulsa Historical Society.*

Seeing the fire, he rushed back to the control room alerting Donley to the fire but not the listening public. Forced by officials to vacate, the two transferred the transmission of the program to a support facility. Moments after they reached Sixth Street, the wooden roof and its supporting girders collapsed, pulling down much of the exterior walls.

KAKC general manager Jim Neal called Avey, who was attending a housewarming party for his only daughter, Pat. Rushing to the scene, he could not bear the sight, saying to a *Tulsa World* reporter, "I've had too many happy memories in that old barn to want to watch it die." He returned to his home at Sixteenth and Gillette.

Turning on the black-and-white television, Avey and his wife tuned in Channel 6. Located only two blocks from the Coliseum, KOTV had set up a camera on the roof of their building and broke into regular programming four times to show the progress of the fire. A stunned Avey sat in front of the tube as the most popular 10:30 p.m. Saturday night show began—ironically, a film of wrestling matches that featured a four-man, tag-team event in Chicago. "I guess I looked at it," Avey told the *World*, "but I don't even remember it. I was too dazed." He wasn't alone.

Among the estimated twelve thousand who quickly gathered to watch the inferno was Tulsa's future hamburger Nazi, J.J. Conley, and his father. Conley remembers his father, who manned the Coliseum lighting system, saying, "Son, you are watching my job go up in smoke."

Fire Marshal Farl Wagner said to the *Tulsa Tribune*, "Presumably, lightning struck the southeast corner of the roof. The wooden roof burned quickly." Within two hours, there was only rubble.

Avey had a $300,000 insurance policy for a building that architects, several years earlier, claimed would take nearly $1.5 million to replace. Following the adjuster's report and settlement, the building was razed and has been a parking lot ever since. Two years ago, daughter Pat reluctantly sold the lot to the East Village development consortium and along with it the sentimental remnants of the Tulsa icon that towered over that parcel of land.

A timepiece and a musical instrument were the only Coliseum survivors. The precision master clock that provides timing signals to synchronize the building's network of slave clocks was being repaired off property. It resides in the Tulsa Historical Society lobby. Suffering significant water damage to its wooden exterior yet restored to its original splendor, the musical survivor was the grand piano originally positioned in the southwest corner of the ground floor, current residence unknown.

Part IV

LANDMARKS AND GANGSTERS:
STREETS, HILLS AND A
MURDEROUS MAESTRO

Chapter 15

THE HILLS HAVE EYES

Standpipe Hill Seldom Stood Still

I climbed the remnants of Standpipe Hill on a recent, windy, early morning with a Wal-Mart canvas chair and a cup of McDonald's coffee. Atop the towering hill immediately north of downtown Tulsa, Turkey Mountain rose nobly in the west, as it did for pioneers and outlaws past. Trains rumbled by several blocks south, but their clickety-clack was lost to me in the din of commuter highway traffic immediately below.

You can see for miles up here, and for blocks: old brick buildings tucked beneath cranes erecting brick replicas. The roof of Brady Theatre looms nearby and, farther, the futuristic metal design of the BOK Center, house of country, rock and the Tulsa Shock.

Several blocks away, unfinished construction borders the original building of Tulsa oilman and philanthropist W.K. Warren, now the Gypsy Coffee House. Guthrie Green, a new entertainment park at Cincinnati and Cameron, stands out. The Greenwood district resurgence beams with the John Hope Franklin Reconciliation Park, laying out an even larger green-venue with statues and benches for contemplation adjacent to ONEOK baseball stadium whose centerfield concession building stands on the ruins of the home of Dick Roland, the falsely accused igniter of the race riot.

The area teems with music venues, business startups and drinking habitués, channeling the days when the railroads came to town a hundred years ago. The scene below Standpipe Hill shows a community familiar with transition.

Known during the pioneering decades of Tulsa as Cherokee Heights, Standpipe Hill became an embittered landmark, a vantage point popular with brigands, supremacists and Pentecostals. The activity perpetrated on its soil gave it a sense of place, a sense of life.

In 1904, when the city tired of toting five-gallon containers of potable water around, a columnar reservoir was constructed with private funding on a mammoth rise between Cincinnati and Main Avenues, rising one hundred feet above the hill top, holding over fifteen thousand gallons of brackish water pumped from the Arkansas River. It looked like an overgrown, black stovepipe, actually called a standpipe tank, hence the name Standpipe Hill.

Above: Standpipe Hill in 1905, shortly after the construction of the water reservoir. *Beryl Ford Collection/Rotary Club and Tulsa Historical Society.*

Below: The morning after the burning of the Greenwood black community adjacent to downtown Tulsa. *Beryl Ford Collection/Rotary Club and Tulsa Historical Societ.*

The railroads passed through town between downtown and Standpipe Hill, bringing thousands of new Tulsans, many of them black, to settle around Standpipe. For nearly two decades, the hill towered over a prosperous and growing community called Greenwood. Things changed as racial tensions within the city escalated, prompting the Tulsa race riot, when an expansive cloud of hazy smoke created by the torching of Greenwood's Black Wall Street buildings on June 1, 1921 shrouded Standpipe Hill north of the battleground. Private planes dropped bombs while the ammo from Oklahoma National Guard machine guns pelleted those hiding on the southern, earthen slope.

The trees of the hill provided defensive positions for besieged, black Tulsans making a last stand. After three days, those not dead or in custody were left to sort the rubble smoldering in the shadow of Standpipe. In the late 1800s, the hill served a more peaceful function.

Hell-bent on getting to church on time, the Dalton gang tied up their horses. From their perch atop the promontory, they scanned the downtown roads of the Indian Territory settlement for any sign of federal marshals and deputized posses. The boys made a deal: Bob, Grat and Emmett Dalton promised local law officials that, within city limits and particularly when worshipping, they would leave one another alone.

With the coast clear, the bandits stashed their binoculars in a sweat-stained saddlebag and made for a little white Methodist church of preacher George Mowbray at the foot of the hill. "They all had wonderful voices," said Hannah Mowbray. They sang in her husband's church on Sundays and ravaged the country during the week.

Heading for the worship service, near the base of the broad hill, they passed the log cabin home, built in 1883, of the first Indian policeman—William Burgess, a Cherokee—who was empowered to apprehend whiskey peddlers and disarm non-citizens unauthorized to carry sidearms. Yet the law looked the other way when the gang strode confidently into stores, cafés and saloons. Three decades later, a popular all-white organization heavily influenced local law enforcement.

The Ku Klux Klan built and occupied a three-story, whitewashed building called Beno Hall by the locals. Situated at the western base of Standpipe Hill on Main Street, just north of Cain's Ballroom, the building, constructed in January 1922 and known officially as the Tulsa Benevolent Association, hosted local politicians, vigilantes and ice cream socials for the teen Klan Klub. Big enough to seat three thousand, it was the social club for

Two ladies in their Sunday best relax on the steps of the Standpipe Hill water reservoir. *Beryl Ford Collection/ Rotary Club and Tulsa Historical Society.*

the vilest Klavern in Oklahoma. In time, the Klan became a fatality of its own violence, diminished in numbers by scandal and disgust, and ultimately sold its property to a church. After a number of businesses occupied the building, radio evangelist Steve Pringle bought the property and renamed it the Evangelistic Temple. "Hallelujahs" washed up its slopes, as if to reclaim the stained soul of Standpipe Hill.

Where years before the Klan terrorized the hill, Pringle preached to his revved-up congregation, drawing the attention of a young preacher from Enid who was ready to burst forth. Oral Roberts, who would come to build a gold-mirrored empire on a fertile bank of the Arkansas River, preached his first tent meeting on the scorched earth adjacent to the Temple in the evening shadows of Standpipe Hill.

When the Reservoir Hill tank became operational in 1926, the old standpipe was demolished. The need to connect Tulsa's community on the north side of the hill with downtown resulted in the bisection of Standpipe Hill, creating north Cincinnati Avenue with the Oklahoma State University–Tulsa campus just east of that thoroughfare in the area originally called Greenwood.

Overgrown with weeds, inhabited by nocturnal transients, pockmarked with broken concrete stairs to nowhere, Standpipe Hill somewhat survives. QuikTrip cups and memories, spent condoms and shell casings lie as proof of purpose.

Chapter 16

ELECTRIC TO ECO TROLLEYS

Champions of Tulsa Transportation

Sitting at the bar in Doe's Eat Place, I gazed up Quincy Street, daydreaming a nostalgic movie reel of an era gone by. The opening scene showed a daybreak shot along a dusty Tulsa street. The year, 1906. I order a Rombauer Zinfandel and a plate of six tamales and let the traffic go through its usual paces. Under the pavement of Fifteenth run the tracks of my musings.

Cherry Street, then; in the early morning, three men wearing coveralls and smoking cigarettes stood on this corner of the dirt-packed streets before punching their time cards. Their clean-faced kids made their way to Longfellow Elementary School at Sixth and Peoria while their wives traveled to a muddy downtown Main Street for a handful of groceries and maybe some headache powders from the drugstore. Families reunited in the late afternoon reversing their morning route to the Brady Heights neighborhood miles away. The options of horse or foot travel were not practical. And the trolleys ran on time.

Rewind: Mass transit in 1906 and beyond linked early-day Tulsans to work, school, stores, parks, theater, recreation and neighboring towns. There were no cars, skateboards or Harley Davidsons.

The trolley rails that ended at Fifteenth and Quincy—where Doe's now grills steaks and shakes cocktails—have been covered with asphalt for decades. Their colorful story involved wild promises, vital connectivity and typical politics.

A growing Tulsey Town demanded suitable infrastructure to support the thousands who were converging on the settlement to work the oil industry.

They needed homes, stores, schools and bars. They needed reliable utilities, and they needed more than horses and wagons. Many knew that Tulsa needed a mass transit system. The solution began as an enticement to an educational institution.

The electric trolley system was a bargaining chip used by land developer Grant C. Stebbins, a founding father of the Tulsa Commercial Club. He used it to persuade Kendall College of Muscogee—a Presbyterian, all-girls school—to relocate its campus to Tulsa. He promised the college's board that if they moved to Tulsa, their institution would enjoy water, utilities and a streetcar depot. Although there was no such transportation option at that time, Stebbins vowed he would make it happen.

The college made the move, setting up classrooms for the future Tulsa University in a local Presbyterian Church while awaiting construction of some buildings and the required utilities on Stebbins's land at Sixth and Delaware. The promised rail system was nowhere in sight.

At first the Tulsa City Council strongly opposed Stebbins's plan, suspecting it as just another utility company conundrum for them to monitor and keep under control. Even though they had no construction materials on hand, Stebbins and his cohorts promised the trolley line would lay track "right down the middle of Main Street" from Tenth to Cameron and agreed to a firm date only a scant sixty days away. With difficulty, Stebbins and his executive crew wrangled the financing for the first arm of their proposed route. Fully expecting the rash promises and aggressive deadlines to fail, the council reluctantly agreed to the 1905 ordinance creating the Tulsa Street Railway (TSR).

Delivery of rails, "rolling stock" (cars) and electric motors was delayed, and it appeared that Stebbins would never meet the two-month goal for setting the first section of track. When the fateful make-or-break day arrived, there were no tracks extending up Main. Undaunted, Stebbins and a few hands laid down several ties at Third and Main. They nailed two borrowed rails to the ties and, having delivered their token of progress, smugly walked away.

The installation of the two rails temporarily placated the council, but the steel tracks were nothing more than Tulsa's first speed bumps endangering the middle of the most traveled intersection in downtown. So that horses, buggies and wagons could again proceed without danger, the tracks were completely covered with dirt.

By 1909, there were TSR electric trolleys traversing up Main Street from Tenth to Cameron and down Frisco to Fifteenth Street, the site of the residential Sophian Plaza. Other routes traveled along North Cheyenne to

A view north on Main Street, showing the new trolley tracks in 1905. *Beryl Ford Collection/ Rotary Club and Tulsa Historical Society.*

the Fairgrounds, the University of Tulsa and several points between. All along the former TSR system are physical reminders of trolley rails buried in shallow graves beneath aging asphalt. Like corpses pushing up to expose their existence, the submerged rails created superficial stress fractures caused by traffic compacting the soft road surface above the unyielding steel rails. Efforts to fill in the crevices with new asphalt created permanent traces of the submerged urban landmarks. The fissures have become memorials to a long-lost time of trolley traffic.

Track scars of one TSR route stop just short of Fifteenth Street on Quincy Avenue, visible from Doe's Eat Place. Several blocks earlier, between Eighth and Tenth Streets, obvious track marks provide evidence of two, side-by-side sets of tracks—passing lanes, if you will—that converged to form a single north and south set of tracks.

TSR was not the only intra-city trolley company transporting Tulsans. A second city trolley company, the Oklahoma Union Traction Co. (OUT), connected Tulsans to popular Orcutt Park on Swan Lake. As passenger-only lines, the two carriers struggled to develop and fund new routes of service. TSR, with its extensive route system, carried significantly larger numbers of people.

Tulsa Street Railway Co. car #455 at the car barn in 1920. *Beryl Ford Collection/Rotary Club and Tulsa Historical Society.*

The gently swaying trolleys connected businesses, schools and citizens. Roaring 1920s Tulsans could make the short trek to an entertainment mecca near the Red Fork community on the west side of the Arkansas River. Opened as Electric Park, it later became Crystal City Park. Pleasure seekers from distant parts of the Tulsa environ rolled past Southwest Boulevard's Howard Park before reaching Crystal City where they could ride the giant roller coaster Zingo that operated at that location until 1937. However, the real attraction was a legendary dance and drink emporium, the Casa Loma, and its legendary terrace. Nestled at the base of Red Fork's Turkey Mountain near the current location of Billy Ray's Barbeque, the Casa Loma supplied the best big bands of the era and attracted people from around the region to dance and misbehave.

For a little spare change, families traveled in comfort to the carnival setting and Ferris wheel at Orcutt Park on Swan Lake or headed north of downtown to Tulsa's first park, Owen Park, named after Tulsa's founding father Chauncey Owen. The park site was originally a dowry awarded to Owen for marrying a local Creek woman.

The trolley routes were so integral to living patterns that new housing developments were often built within proximity of existing routes. With rumors that an arm of the route close to their home might be discontinued, families made decisions to move closer to a more reliable extension. The development of more trolley systems near Tulsa created a network of active railways with adjacent cities. Yet troubling events were on the horizon.

For twenty years, TSR linked citizens to neighborhoods, parks, entertainment and commerce. By 1923, it had twenty-one miles of track and fifty-two cars. The banner year of 1916 showed a profit of over $1.2 million by 2010 standards, but the advent of World War I and its resulting inflation was a blow to the intra-city trolley lines.

For six of those twenty years, people got around on "jitneys," used Fords with running boards, "jit," meaning nickel, the price of a ride. A jitney could carry up to eleven passengers along established trolley routes, challenging and nearly financially crippling TSR.

The advent of Henry Ford's affordable Model T and small, comfortable buses sealed the fate of Tulsa streetcars. Trolley pioneer Tulsa Street Railway made its last run in 1926 while the romantic adventure of electric trolley passenger travel on the OUT came to a halt in 1935.

Cherry Street, now: the dream ends, the reel spins with the rapid, flapping sound of celluloid jarring me out of a past made pleasant by my own pondering. I step back into the evening, the light of Doe's bar yellowing the sidewalk. So many lights, and the nights will never be as dark as they once were.

A bus rumbles down Fifteenth, fueled by natural gas. A ride is a $1.50, half that for those with disabilities or on Medicare. But I have a car, and I get into it and drive the several blocks home, alone.

Chapter 17

CEDAR STREET

Tulsa's Proudest Thoroughfare

In the early 1970s, an eighteen-year-old Lebanese immigrant trekked down the sidewalks of Sixth Street from his West Tulsa apartment to the University of Tulsa. As he crossed Peoria each day, the student traveled where thousands of Tulsa pioneers had walked before. The decayed string of Plains Commercial–style buildings gave little clue as to the ghosts of the street's historical past.

Khaled "K." Rahal came to Tulsa with mixed feelings.

"It was not a happy time—I did not want to be here," he said. "In Lebanon I was to start law school while at the University of Tulsa, I was a freshman. I was afraid I had made a mistake."

His economic future was as uncertain and undefined as the city itself.

The story of Sixth Street began soon after the 1901 discovery of oil in Red Fork just across the Arkansas River. Manufacturing and industrial businesses developed north of Sixth within sight of the groaning railroads near downtown. Determined to avoid the economic trap of being a one-industry town, a civic Commercial Club offered monetary bonuses and partial moving expenses to attract manufacturing companies. By 1911, the factory area included a glass company and a cotton oil business, as well as a canning company and a broom factory.

By 1910, both sides of Sixth Street supported flourishing businesses: a blacksmith, a machine shop, various oil companies and related businesses, a wire fence warehouse and several lumberyards. Sixth Street was taking shape.

With the annexation of the area east of downtown, Tulsa doubled in size to twenty thousand. East–west streets in the new district were named after trees, and the main street along their western origins was Pearl Street. Continuing the established Tulsa downtown format of numbered streets and eastern U.S. cities, Cedar Street became Sixth, and Pearl became Peoria.

From Sixth and Peoria eastward, businesses replaced residences and provided the needed infrastructure for the exploding population. The Colonial Grocery and rival Barrel Food Grocers were side by side. A confectioner plied his trade as the Dixie Bar down the block served thirsty patrons celebrating the end of the workday.

Bill and Bud's Phillips 66 gas station on the northeast corner of Peoria shared the north side of the avenue with a café, a barbershop, a drugstore and a garage. The hardworking population crowded the stores and shops along the corridor.

An ingenious scheme to finance the purchase of the land for Tulsa's first Factory Addition just north of Sixth included an auction of 135 lots. A *Tulsa Daily Democrat* ad promoting the auction offered "every fifth lady buying a lot a five dollar dress pattern and to every fifth gentleman a five dollar hat."

Metal workers, carpenters and clerks working in neighboring industries lived in the houses on these parcels. New workers poured into the neighborhood. The influx of their children and increasing numbers of births prompted the construction of Longfellow School in 1913.

Several blocks before Sixth intersects with Lewis, a building stands that once housed George Wallace's Oklahoma Presidential campaign headquarters. Across the street is a former residence of the Perryman family, prominent Creek settlers whose land holdings became downtown Tulsa.

Not much farther east of Lewis was the site of a bustling open-air lumberyard, where two brothers in the 1920s erected a commercial ice-making house. Frosted plumes escaped heavenwards from the ventilation system as locals rolled up to the west loading dock to cart off ice. Tulsa Ice Co. employees slid hefty ice blocks into delivery trucks. Eventually, advances in refrigeration put the icehouse out of business and the building became a warehouse. Today, the reknowned Selser Schaefer Architects firm occupies the historic structure.

Although pedestrian traffic dominated Sixth, people also boarded horse-driven trolleys and, later, the Tulsa Street Railroad trolleys connecting residential areas to factories and shopping venues. Removed for scrap metal during World War I, trolley life disappeared.

The former ice building is now Selser Schaefer Architects. *Author collection.*

"Sixth Street is a uniquely Tulsa mixture of bootstrap, self-made identities with freewheeling ambitions and personal respect," says Dean Williams, a Sixth Street resident. "It seems especially American to me."

Williams has a point: you can read America's story simply by looking at Sixth. During the Great Depression, businesses evaporated, and the financial distress decimated the once teeming shops. After World War II, the migration to the suburbs nearly emptied the densely populated district. Automobiles became part of every family unit, and mobility was no longer limited to rail transportation or foot travel. Shopping centers with convenient parking changed Tulsans' habits. Life along Sixth crumbled. Blight overtook the once proud thoroughfare.

K. Rahal has owned the Eclipse bar and music venue at Sixth and Quaker for decades, as well as a diner that was his first acquisition. Rahal became fascinated with this area forty years ago, "long before I could afford to buy a soda pop."

The old bar next door to his diner became available, and he bought it.

"My dream started to come to life," he says.

Rahal firmly believes the time for Sixth Street has finally arrived, and he has a plan in place. He is not alone.

More than a decade ago, a band of locals formed the Sixth Street Neighborhood Association. Five years later, the group reorganized as the Pearl

Khaled Rahal in front of his Eclipse nightclub on Sixth Street. *Author collection.*

District Association, made up of dedicated Tulsans who defined the organization's mission as "reinventing the art of city life in Tulsa."

After years of planning, changes are in store for the west end of Sixth. A retention pond called the West Pearl Pond will corral storm water to eliminate flood zone concerns. Dramatic improvements to the Sixth and Peoria intersection and several blocks east of Peoria will help transform Sixth Street into a "living street" that makes it more pedestrian oriented. Using newly designed building codes, proposed plans create pedestrian-friendly spaces, including a water canal and a brick street that will be well situated for special events, outdoor dining and music.

Shelby Navarro and his wife, Rachel, are part of that plan. He's an architect with downtown renovation credits, and Rachel works with him as a certified public accountant. Among their other Pearl District business interests is the ornate building on Sixth at Quaker, constructed by Everett House in the early 1920s. A wine bar and art shop are slated to open in what was formerly a corner drugstore.

The Navarros also own the building across the street on the corner of Sixth and Peoria. Tulsa Councilman and Restaurateur Blake Ewing—a Blue Dome District kingpin—will soon open a new dining spot: the Phoenix.

The restaurant's name fits. Like the mythological bird that rose from the fiery ashes, Sixth Street, for too long a stained symbol of the past, is poised to regain its splendor.

Shelby Navarro smiles as he confesses, "It's a beautiful nighttime sight to look west down Sixth Street."

Chapter 18

"CREEPY" KARPIS AND THE CENTRAL PARK GANG

D ental records proved the badly decomposed body that washed up on the Crystal Beach shores of Ontario, minus hands and feet, to be twenty-nine-year-old crime-boss physician, Joseph P. Moran, M.D. of Chicago.

So that one bad guy, Alvin "Creepy" Karpis, could not be traced to abandoned hotel rooms and cars, Moran had injected Karpis's fingers with cocaine and successfully scraped off his fingerprints. The doctor also helped launder a portion of the $200,000 ransom money for St. Paul banker Edward Bremmer. While drinking heavily with the gang at the Casino Club outside Toledo one evening, he bragged, "I have you guys in the palm of my hand."

Later that night, Moran disappeared. Authorities claimed Tulsan Fred Barker and Karpis had taken him night fishing on Lake Erie.

On May 1, 1936, a Friday, FBI director J. Edgar Hoover hurried to catch a plane for New Orleans to make the arrest of Tulsa gangster—and Public Enemy No. 1—Alvin "Creepy" Karpis. As Hoover landed, an execution team of twenty-six federal agents formed a web around a Jefferson Parkway building where they knew Karpis was hiding. Unexpectedly, Karpis and one Freddie Hunter sauntered out of the building and climbed into their car. Alvin, called "Creepy" by his friends, got behind the wheel.

Agents quickly surrounded the automobile, with two Feds lying on the hood pointing their Tommy guns directly at the occupants. The situation was well in hand when Hoover was encouraged to approach the driver-side window. The only "collar" of his career involved ordering the handcuffs be placed on Karpis. Only there were none. The G-men were armed for a murderous shootout, not an arrest. The nation's most notorious criminal—wanted for murder in fourteen states—was cuffed with an agent's necktie and taken prisoner.

It was fitting that the evil and deadly Karpis would spend the next three decades in the most vile and dangerous federal penitentiary, Alcatraz, the infamous "Rock," as Prisoner 325. Arriving in a Fort Leavenworth train car with twenty other hardened criminals—including former Tulsa Central Park gang member and criminal compadre Harry Campbell—their railcar cellblock was shunted onto a long pier jutting out into San Francisco Bay.

"Take a good look, you bastards," the huge, uniformed guard yelled to the shackled residents of the launch as it bounced through the chilly, fifty-degree waves. Up ahead, dozens of guards armed with riot guns, heavy rifles and Thompson submachine guns lined a catwalk along the perilous cliffs below the three-story, maximum-security prison that housed America's most irredeemable criminals.

It was going to be "old home" week for Karpis. Awaiting his arrival, Tulsa hoodlums Volney Davis, Harry Sawyer and Doc Barker, the third son of the infamous "Ma" Barker, were already suited up with Alcatraz "heavy

wool" long johns and coveralls with their name and Alcatraz prisoner number sewn on.

Having graduated to the major-league crime scene from the bad-boy incubator of Sixth Street and Peoria Avenue, Tulsa's Central Park Gang was reunited on the Rock. During their formative years, these burglars and highway robbers terrorized the neighborhood and met in the then-sprawling Pearl District park. The park served as a boardroom and storage facility for stolen goods and explosives.

Central Park has come a long way. The Sixth Street landmark of Longfellow Elementary across from the park was the educational home to many gang

"Creepy" Karpis poses for his first Alcatraz mug shot. *www.fbi.gov.*

members. In its place stands the Indian Health Care Resource Center. The grounds of the once heavily treed green space that was Tulsa's first park now feature a senior recreation center and a large tract of high-dollar brownstones. The tranquil beauty of the pond and water treatment soothes the former hotbed of derring-do nine decades gone.

In the early 1920s, a patrol officer discovered a small tent pitched in Central Park that contained twenty-six pairs of stolen shoes. The petty thieves included five gangsters, the oldest only seventeen, who were quickly detained. Later uncovered by park beat cops, gang members a little further up the crime chain had hidden a stockpile of dynamite and nitroglycerin, intended to blow the doors on the National Guard Armory across the street. The expected bounty was shotguns and pistols.

The young toughs became newspaper legends for their dangerous holdups of cars on main Tulsa thoroughfares as well as daylight petty burglaries. Their guns intimidated scores of city innocents during a decade-long reign.

Sixteen-year-old gang member Eva Jacobs—known in the tabloids as the "bandit queen"—and several male hoods stopped a family sedan on a downtown street. Forced from their car at gunpoint, the victims handed over their valuables before being brusquely thrown back into their vehicle.

Eva and her thugs successfully terrorized motorists for months. Newspapers reported the police were powerless to stop the nightmare of these "stick-up artists," adding, "Unfortunate wayfarers were held at the points of pistols and robbed of their belongings, [and] citizens cringed in their homes."

According to the September 3, 1922 morning edition of the *Tulsa Tribune*, Little Eva and her teenage crew were finally captured, thus reducing the threat of byway holdups and the danger of their weapons. Yet, the Tulsa crime scene swelled its ranks.

It was into this scene that Karpis came. He was born Alvin Raymond Karpis in 1908 to Lithuanian immigrants in Montreal. The family subsequently moved to Chicago, where young Alvin was diagnosed with a "leaky heart" and advised to move to quieter surroundings. He was shipped to an aunt in Topeka, Kansas, where by age ten, he owned his first gun and was running errands for local pimps and other crime figures. He began a life of crime, he told a biographer, because "that's where the action was."

Nicknamed for a sinister smile that rode below a pair of dark, stone-cold eyes of pure evil, "Creepy" Karpis came to Tulsa late in the Central Park Gang saga. He met Fred Barker, son of Tulsa resident Arizona "Ma" Kate Barker, while serving time in the Kansas State Prison. After their release in the spring of 1931, they came to Tulsa, where the cool and handsome

Karpis met a downtown Bishop's cafeteria worker, Dorothy Slayman. He told her he was a jewelry salesman, and they married.

Later in 1931, Barker and Karpis—employing the alias of "George Haller"—were back in business. The pair robbed a jewelry store and was arrested. Barker was never charged and soon released. Oddly, Karpis, who entered a guilty plea, had his four-year sentence overturned when the loot from the heist was returned. Free again, both fled to Missouri.

Several days later, the two robbed a store in West Plains, Missouri. Sheriff C.R. Kelly and a deputy named Kurt spotted the pair and approached their car to investigate.

"I was with Sheriff Kelly when we found the Ma Barker Gang," Kurt was reported saying. "They knew it was us when Kelly opened the door. Bullets came out of the blue DeSoto. Then the DeSoto went out of the garage and got away. Sheriff Kelly was dead!"

Deciding against a return to Tulsa, Barker and Karpis headed for Minneapolis to hide out with the now-legendary "Ma" Barker. He never returned to his marital bungalow at the northwest corner of Brady Street and Boston Avenue. Filing for divorce in 1935, Slayman claimed she had not seen him for four years. He was on the road a lot, raking in non-taxable revenue and leaving a bloody trail.

The Central Park gang kept up its antics. "Curley" Davis enters the pages of history in a tag-team effort with rising star Fred Barker and fellow Central Parker Howard Musgrave. Davis worked as a water boy at the St. John Hospital building site and put his inside knowledge to use organizing a burglary of some equipment. During the heist, night watchman Thomas Sherrill discovered the intruders. Davis wheeled and emptied his revolver into the undermatched Sherrill and killed him.

While serving a life sentence for the Sherrill murder—a stay that involved multiple escapes and recaptures—Davis was granted a twenty-month leave of absence from the state pen at McAlester. Karpis claimed the state's decision was greased with his $1,500 bribe. Davis chose not to return to prison; instead, he took up with the Karpis-Barker gang to successfully rob numerous banks.

The gang was poised for its most complicated and lucrative undertaking. Following the successful, maiden kidnapping of Minnesota beer magnate William J. Hamm Jr. and the collection of a $100,000 ransom, Karpis set in motion the abduction of banker Bremmer. It proved to be the demise of the remaining Barker family, Karpis and all their henchmen.

Needing more manpower, Karpis headed for Tulsa to recruit colleagues from the hoodlum pool at Sixth and Peoria. Although the Barker hideout at

401 North Cincinnati Avenue occasionally provided him refuge on his visits to Tulsa, Karpis usually bunked with the notorious George "Burrhead" Keady, an agent of sorts for local petty criminals. Harry Campbell, a Keady find, was an oilfield thief before becoming Karpis's right-hand man.

Nicknamed "Limpy" for a bum leg, Campbell was first arrested at age sixteen for burglary and larceny. After an escape from the Tulsa County jail, he was incarcerated for some bank burglaries in which he used nitroglycerin. Karpis liked his credentials.

Tulsans Harry Sawyer, William Weaver and Cassius McDonald teamed up with buddies Davis and Campbell to become a part of the Karpis-Barker gang's Minnesota rampage that included the fateful kidnapping and successful ransoming of Bremmer. Netting $200,000 in marked bills, the gang split up to launder the proceeds in Cuba, Chicago and Reno and lay low. Yet by 1936, they had all been convicted in the Bremmer case and were at Alcatraz when Karpis arrived from New Orleans via Fort Leavenworth.

When the gang separated after splitting the Bremmer ransom, Karpis returned to Toledo, Ohio, where he settled into a house with his moll of three years, Dolores Delaney. Early in their liaison, Karpis arranged and paid for the sixteen-year-old to abort their love child. In 1935, she was pregnant again when the Feds traced Karpis and Campbell, along with their female companions, to the Dan-Mor rooming house in Atlantic City, New Jersey.

Blasting their way out, Karpis and Campbell shot a policeman in the face and wounded several others. Errantly shot in the leg by Campbell, Delaney was nabbed, arrested and charged for her complicity in the Bremmer kidnapping. She was temporarily moved to Philadelphia, where the child she conceived with Karpis—a son—was born.

Returned to court, Delaney ultimately received a five-year sentence for harboring Karpis. The two lovers never saw each other again, and his parents, Mr. and Mrs. John Karpowicz of Chicago, adopted the infant, christening him Raymond Alvin Karpowicz. Karpis spent time in Chicago, but business always came before family.

In 1958, while imprisoned in Fort Leavenworth for a few months, his twenty-three-year-old son and new bride paid a surprise visit to Karpis. "Then I seen them," Karpis remembered in his autobiography, On the Rock, co-authored with Robert Livesey and released in 1980. "It is as if I am looking at myself in the mirror," he continued. The presence of a special guard during their visit infuriated the younger Ray, and the guard ended the visit. On the way out, Karpis's son lost his temper with the warden, resulting in his permanent banishment from the facility. Fort Leavenworth also did not want his father there. Karpis was returned to Alcatraz.

Determined to stay clear of other prisoners' problems, he vowed his remaining time on the island was just for him. Sitting in his cell across from the barbershop, Karpis learned to play a steel guitar. Shortly after his transfer to McNeil Island in Puget Sound, Washington, where he would be paroled, Karpis met a quiet, meek inmate named "Little Charlie," a devout believer in the Church of Scientology. He begged to learn the instrument. Preferring "rock 'n roll" songs to Karpis's country western, Charlie mastered it quickly. Charlie later became infamous as Charles Manson.

In 1973, four years after being paroled and seeking peaceful refuge, Karpis moved to the sunny Spanish Riviera city of Torrelimos. He worked on the Rock book beside the pool at Sofico while amusing himself with a series of girlfriends. Yet some of his thoughts smacked of yesteryear.

In an odd criminal salvo, Ray planned an imaginary robbery of the Banco Coca near his apartment in Spain. The "perfect score," he explained to author Livesey, were the two side-by-side banks teeming with money during the tourist season. Easy to break in at night and empty both vaults. Bada-bing, bada-boom.

With no regrets or remorse for past actions, Karpis claimed Alcatraz did nothing to reform him.

Chapter 19

FIDDLER SPADE COOLEY
PLAYED ROUGH

His Photo Terrorizes Patrons of Cain's Ballroom

On a furlough from a California state prison, convicted wife killer Spade Cooley walked off the stage of Oakland's Paramount Theatre, basking in the thunderous applause of 2,800 Western swing aficionados who'd come to see the former fiddle star turned inmate. Anchoring the first half of the show with his three-song set, a beaming Spade raised his violin above his head, saluting the cheering crowd. Their jubilation continued as he disappeared behind the curtain, made a comment to waiting friends and suddenly slumped to the dressing room floor. Then he died, to a standing ovation.

Part Cherokee, Donnell Cooley was born into a family of fiddlers on February 22, 1910, in a tornado cellar on a dusty ranch near Grand in western Oklahoma. Today, Grand twists in the wind, a ghost town with only the footings of the courthouse and its vault showing above the red dirt. Even then, it didn't offer enough to hold Cooley.

At the age of twenty-one, Cooley lit for California, arriving in Modesto with "a nickel in my pocket and a fiddle under my arm." Cooley became a farm laborer, nighttime fiddler and card gambler. He claimed he couldn't see himself "farting down a row of beans," preferring instead a future in Hollywood westerns, studio recordings and radio shows. Playing cards one night, he drew three straight flushes, all of 'em spades, and was ever after known as "Spade" Cooley. Feeling lucky, he left for Los Angeles.

Thanks to the scores of 1930s Dust Bowl immigrants heading down Route 66 to the Golden State, honky-tonks and cowboy dance halls became the rage on the West Coast, with the likes of Cooley and the Sons of the Pioneers supplying the tunes. Their brand of music was western swing, characterized by a southwestern-bred hybrid of folk, bluegrass, hillbilly, swing and jazz.

Spade ruled the West Coast Western swing era. He was challenged by Bob Wills, who brought his Texas Playboys to Los Angeles to make a play for Spade's steady gig at Bert Phillips's Venice Pier Ballroom. A battle of the bands took place on the pier, with thousands crowding onto the huge dock. Ever the bulldog, Spade crowed that he'd "show who was the king in this here sunny state." Spade won and thereafter proclaimed himself the "King of Western Swing."

With his bandleader style, Cooley was a Benny Goodman in cowboy duds. Likewise, he suited his dozen band members in $500, custom-made western wear and gave them spiced-up nicknames like Deuce, Cactus and Smokey. Wills stuck to the old-fashioned band configuration that often included horns and the more traditional get-up of cowboy suits and neckerchief ties. But more than clothes separated their styles.

Shelby Eicher is bandleader of the Tulsa Playboys, a Western swing band playing monthly at Cain's Ballroom in downtown Tulsa, where an over-sized photo of Spade looks down on the crowd. Eicher, ever a student of swing music, said:

> There are fundamental differences between Spade's and Bob's music. Bob had a foot squarely in the blues world and allowed the fiddles to draw more on their ethnic fiddle-tune style. Spade arranged his fiddle section to have a more violin quality.
>
> The other great difference to my ear is that Bob had access to great songs, many written by Cindy Walker. Spade's material was a little tongue in cheek, and this may have been due to his work in Hollywood. Both men had great bands and were somewhat bigger-than-life characters. Bob Wills had a charisma in my opinion comparable to Elvis Presley which is a valuable quality that set him apart and added to his legendary status.

For a time, Spade and Wills shared Tulsa's O.W. Mayo as a manager and confidant. Both played the storied Cain's Ballroom in downtown Tulsa where the historic forum displays oversized photos of western swing and country stars. From his perch high above the dance floor, Spade's menacing smile shines down on Tulsa's Cain's Ballroom revelers. Along with his signature, he gives a shout out to Mayo. Wills's portrait seems timid and country.

Both held dear to the whiskey bottle and paid for it. Wills was known as a binge drinker who'd miss entire performances due to his drinking. He

Spade Cooley photo hangs along the perimeter of Tulsa's famous Cain's Ballroom. *Author collection.*

suffered several heart attacks before dying of a stroke in 1975. With his huge success going to his head, Spade was always difficult to handle, but his near-constant drinking made him a devil and a half. And his bent toward physical brutality made him a feared man.

Shortly after Cooley's "Shame on You" hit No. 1 on the country charts, Missouri clarinetist Ella Mae Evans sat in with the band. Despite the pleading of manager Bobbie Bennett, who protested, "She had no voice," Cooley made the blonde-haired, brown-eyed Evans his lead singer. He liked to introduce her on stage as "the purtiest little filly in California." They soon married, and not long after, her short vocal career ended with the birth of Melody in 1946 and Donnell Jr. in 1948. Cooley retired her and the kids to his Mojave ranch house.

His career, meanwhile, was about to go meteoric. The "Spade Cooley Time" on KFVD radio in LA became a staple of southern California airwaves. Not long after, Cooley began starring in his own syndicated TV show. Appearing in nearly fifty B-westerns for Republic Studios, Spade usually played bit parts that often showcased his band. He became a local celebrity in a city full of them and enjoyed the trappings of stardom. He'd loan his fifty-six-foot yacht to Roy and Dale Rogers, who'd take family fishing trips to Catalina Island. His closets were lined with one hundred custom cowboy suits, fifty hats and three dozen pairs of boots. All told, Cooley was bringing in $10,000 a week (about $120,000 today).

But Cooley's drinking was getting the better of him. He drank and fired band members in moments of drunken anger. He got fired from his television show after a ten-year run, at least in part due to his drinking. Things hit rock bottom in 1956, when the radio station cut him loose.

Cooley combined the booze with a pathological jealousy. He convinced himself that Ella Mae was sleeping around. He confessed his love for her, hoping for reassurance. She sat quietly, offering no rebuttal or consolation. With no concrete proof of her straying, Spade became delusional about her betrayals.

His stock continued to plummet when rock 'n' roll came in and danced on the grave of western swing. The recording contracts, studio calls and concert bookings dwindled to nothing by 1960. With a reported $15 million in the bank, the little man with the big talent redirected his entrepreneurial ambition to real-estate development.

Licking his wounds, Cooley left his Encino townhouse on fabled Ventura Boulevard and moved in with Ella Mae and the kids, whom he'd kept cooped up all those years at the ranch. Living there put him closer to his new venture, Water Worldland, a project aiming to cash in on the success of the 1955 opening of Disneyland. Cooley envisioned an eighty-acre park with a lake for boat races, fishing, shops, a big swimming pool and a set for television production.

Being closer to his wife made it easier for Spade to keep track of her movements. Through his alcohol haze, every man was her potential lover. Interrogating her every moment, demanding she confess her extramarital affairs, he abused her, first with words and later with fists.

By this time in 1961, Cooley began chasing his whiskey shots with uppers in the morning and downers after nighttime boozing. He became disoriented and wildly abusive, forcing Ella Mae to send the kids away to live with a nearby friend.

Ella Mae was in a local hospital recovering from a hysterectomy when Spade caught her on the phone with another man. "So what?" she said. "Now you know." Cooley asked a Wonderland associate if he know anything about Ella Mae misbehaving. He told him of a man called Bud Davenport and took him to his trailer home in Granada Park.

Cooley confronted Davenport, who gave nothing but guff, so Spade smacked him in the kisser. When he got home and phoned Ella Mae's room, she wouldn't take his call. He called a friend and nurse, Dorothy Davis, and begged her to tell his wife, "I love her with all my heart."

Ella Mae came home, and for a time, things were calm. It wasn't long, though, before the physical and emotional outrage reached new levels, for both of them. Plied with pills and booze, their thoughts became muddled, adding to the tension. They went back and forth about divorcing, with Ella alternately digging in her heels and then yielding. For her trouble, Spade gave her a beating. Then he'd sober up and say how much he loved her. Finally, Ella Mae cracked.

They went for a drive and a long talk. Angling for a divorce, Ella Mae confessed to giving a man named Bud Campbell $600 because, "I thought I was in love with him." Spade drove on, numb from the drugs, the drink and the pain. Docile and strangely serene, he swung the car away from the desert toward the Pacific Ocean. As the car rolled to a stop, a tired peace washed over them.

Leaving the car, they approached the edge of the three-hundred-foot cliff, hand-in-hand. Far below, the crashing waves beat out a hypnotic rhythm. The end to their hell seemed close, yet, their demons were not ready for them. They backed away from the precipice, returning to the car, locating a motel for a kiss-and-makeup session that both knew was not going to heal the wounds.

Back on the highway, she restated her conviction for divorce. Ella Mae demanded he drive her to her parents in North Hollywood, and Spade acquiesced.

He pulled up to the house, and she got out of the car, alone. A confused Cooley rolled down the window to say goodbye but, instead, begged her for a second chance. Tormented by the powers of love and drugs, Ella Mae climbed back in the car.

He headed for home. Disconsolate over what might be in store, Ella Mae pushed open her door and leaped from the moving car. "I just want to die," she told Spade, who held her in his arms. "I just want to die."

He wanted to drive her to a hospital but she refused. They went back to the house that was no longer a home, its rooms strewn with half-eaten hamburgers, rotting apple cores and multiple pill bottles on the bed stand—pills for tension, pills for nerves, sleeping pills and phenobarbital.

The next morning, Cooley tried in vain to get back to work. He paced anxiously between drinks. Martin, his only remaining associate, took note of Cooley's bruised hands, which looked more like those of a street fighter than a fiddler. Ella Mae walked into the room wearing a dirty robe, her face discolored and in obvious pain, and slumped into a chair.

Martin knew he had been beating her. Disgusted, he left the house. "I can tell you things now," she said, raising her eyes toward Cooley.

She began with Davenport, of how she'd become a recruit for his free-love cult near Los Angeles. Cooley responded by yelling, his anger ricocheting off the walls. Drunk out of his mind, Cooley went off on Ella Mae.

Fourteen-year-old Melody walked in the house around 6:00 p.m. A blood-splattered Cooley met her at the door. "You're going to watch me kill her," he said, pointing a gun between her eyes. "If you don't, I'll kill you, too. I'll kill us all."

Ella Mae lay still on the carpet. "We'll see if she is dead," he said. Bending down, he touched his burning cigarette to her skin not once but twice. She didn't move or make a sound.

The phone rang. As Cooley turned to pick up the receiver, Melody ran out the door. He had called several friends to come to the house, telling them Ella Mae was hurt. Eventually, he phoned for an ambulance. Five hours had gone by. As she was loaded onto a stretcher, the driver recalled Cooley saying, "I love you. Please, don't be dead."

The coroner reported that Ella Mae had strangulation bruises and deep, dark contusions on many parts of her body. She died from blood gushing out of a ruptured aorta. Cooley was formally charged with first-degree murder. At trial, the prosecutor called it a "murder by torture" involving stomping, beating and strangling.

Following weeks of testimony and a break to treat Spade for a heart attack, a jury convicted him on August 19, 1961. Cooley, against his attorney's recommendation, withdrew his insanity plea, opening the door to a possible execution. Instead, the judge sentenced him to life in prison, which ordinarily meant the forbidding, hard-time San Quentin. But, with his long history of heart problems, Cooley was assigned to the medical ward of the California state prison at Vacaville, just east of Napa Valley, while daughter Melody, some say, moved in with relatives in the Tulsa suburb of Broken Arrow.

Cooley became a model prisoner, found religion, built fiddles in the hobby shop and taught inmates to play. By 1965, he began to show contrition for his wife's murder. In 1966, Ronald Reagan became governor of California. In the 1950s, he'd appeared on Spade's TV shows numerous times. "It seemed like only yesterday those two were clowning around and laughing it up backstage," remembered Bobbie Bennett, Cooley's manager.

A mutual friend in the B-movie business asked Reagan to pardon Cooley. Reagan balked at an official pardon, but the California parole board unanimously recommended Cooley's parole for February 22, 1970, his sixtieth birthday. Reagan signed the special release papers, telling Bennett he was "repaying an old debt."

Arcade card for Spade Cooley. *Author collection.*

Four months before his release, Reagan authorized an interim release allowing Cooley to travel to Oakland to make his first public appearance in nine years. Heading for what he thought was a concert for other inmates, Cooley lit up another cigarette and shuffled out of his elaborately furnished private cell at the Vacaville prison, wearing a borrowed suit several sizes too large. He entered a surprise party thrown for him by high-up prison officials and his former manager Bennett. A bigger surprise was being escorted to a black limousine.

Only told he was playing for an outside benefit, the bewildered Cooley arrived an hour later at the back door of a large auditorium in a jam-packed parking lot. "Must be rasslin' night," Spade said. Escorted to a small dressing room with a pencil drawn sign scrawled with a misspelled "Cooly" taped to the door, he changed into one of his old, high-dollar band suits Bennett laid out for him.

"Two minutes to show time, Mr. Cooley," a stagehand yelled through the door. "Okay, son. It's a deal," he replied, sweating and scraping nicotine off his front teeth and upper lip. Spade, Bennett and his old pal and emcee for the event, Chill Wills, walked to the curtain together.

An offstage announcer introduced Wills, who strolled out to center stage. "Y'all fasten up yer stirrups and cinch-down yer saddles," he growled, "'cause y'all 'bout to take 'nother wild ride with our good ol' fiddlin' friend, the King of Western Swing, Spade Cooley!"

A stunned Spade stepped onto that Oakland stage to play in the "Grand Old Opry Spectacular" benefitting a local sheriff's association. Prior to his first note, Spade thanked the deputies for "the chance to be free for a while." The sold-out auditorium cheered the three songs Cooley played with the twenty-four-piece band, including "Fidoolin," a "San Antonio Rose" tribute to Bob Wills and his signature closer, "Shame on You."

Leaving the stage to thunderous applause, he greeted friends and reporters behind the curtain. "I think it is going to work out for me," he said.

With the standing ovation ringing in his ears, he retired to his dressing room to change out of his sweat-laden suit. When he failed to make a curtain call, Wills and Bennett forced open the door. Cooley was naked, sprawled out on the dirty concrete floor where he'd collapsed, holding the broken fiddle neck in one hand and a picture of Ella Mae and him in the other.

Wills announced to the audience that there would be no second half of the show. As the band struck up the sad cowboy dirge, "Goin' Home," Chill Wills told the hushed crowd, "Spade Cooley, is…is, well, podnahs, he's dead."

BIBLIOGRAPHY

All essays except "The White Knight Vigilantes" were originally published by This Land Press, Tulsa, Oklahoma, thislandpress.org.

ABOUT THE AUTHOR

S teve Gerkin is a native Iowan and retired from his thirty-six-year general dentistry practice in 2010. He has been published numerous times in the magazine *This Land* (Tulsa), for which he is a contributing editor. In addition to wine-related articles in an international wine and cuisine magazine, *Gastronome*, Steve is a university-level wine educator, a regional cuisine and wine lecturer and a French wine scholar.

Steve and his wife, Sue, live in Tulsa, Oklahoma.

Printed in the USA
CPSIA information can be obtained
at www.ICGtesting.com
LVHW022111261023
762249LV00004B/27